Faustina Hasse Hodges

Edward Hodges

Faustina Hasse Hodges

Edward Hodges

ISBN/EAN: 9783337177041

Printed in Europe, USA, Canada, Australia, Japan

Cover: Foto ©ninafisch / pixelio.de

More available books at **www.hansebooks.com**

EDWARD HODGES

DOCTOR IN MUSIC OF SYDNEY SUSSEX COLLEGE, CAMBRIDGE
ORGANIST OF THE CHURCHES OF ST. JAMES AND
ST. NICHOLAS, BRISTOL, ENGLAND, 1819-1838
ORGANIST AND DIRECTOR IN TRINITY
PARISH, NEW YORK, 1839-1859

BY HIS DAUGHTER

FAUSTINA H. HODGES

"Clarum et venerabile nomen"

G. P. PUTNAM'S SONS

NEW YORK   LONDON
27 WEST TWENTY-THIRD STREET   24 BEDFORD STREET STRAND
The Knickerbocker Press
1896

The Knickerbocker Press, New York

NOTE.

MISS FAUSTINA HASSE HODGES, eldest daughter of the late Dr. Edward Hodges, herself a gifted musician and organist, had in preparation for many years a memoir of her Father, " the founder and illustrious representative of the Anglican cathedral school of music in the American Church." Miss Hodges died in 1895, before completing her labor of love, and from the mass of material she had collected, the following selections have been made by Miss E. Dodds, at the request of the Executors.

The work has been revised by her brother, the Rev. J. Sebastian B. Hodges, D.D., Rector of St. Paul's Church, Baltimore, and is now published as her loving tribute to the memory of her Father.

New York, April, 1896.

CONTENTS.

Contents

ILLUSTRATIONS.

Faustina Hasse Hodges.

PREFACE.

THIS book is in no sense a life-narrative, but is merely meant to preserve in vivid colouring and freshness some of the marked events of my Father's life; and more especially the striking individualities of his character, with the impressions they created on the lives and minds of those with whom he came in contact; running through all, the golden thread of his musical life and work, yet without being an approach to a scientific account of his musical career.

It is supported by facts taken from his early journals and a few letters, until my own memory takes up the subject—a subject to which I can never do justice. I have written as an *observer*, as a *musician*, and as a *daughter;* but in all these I must fall short.

Having touched upon my Father's diaries, I must go on to say that, above and beyond their being absolutely astonishing as to their size and number, they are equally so as specimens of beautiful writing—ready for the press as they leave his hand, perfect in diction, refined, often classic in style, and all in marginal, indexical, and datal order.

And they present *a Life;* his life.

Beginning at fifteen, after the "translation" of his father, a hard, rational, boyish, practical life of work, diligence, and thought ; steering clear of evil, adhering to good.

Life, evincing strength of purpose, steadfastness in religious principles ; regular observance of Sunday, and thoughtful attention to sermons.

Life in emotion, religious and passionate ; life in effort, surmounting difficulties ; life in progress, in music, in reading, in study, in observation, in scientific research, in inexhaustible power and generality of invention.

Life in practical philosophy. Life in politics, as embracing duty to man, to his country, and to his sovereign.

Life in adversity, in resistance to temptation ; in social enjoyment and mental elevation.

Life in sorrow and loss.

Life as a battle-ground.

Life in its highest aspirations ; life as a probation.

Life in hope, in patience (which never failed), in tribulation, in faith, in trust and resignation ; and in and through all these : LIFE IN VICTORY.

In studying my Father's life, one must be struck with the variety and versatility of his powers, and the thorough-going earnestness with which he followed up any one of them. His knowledge was never allowed to remain superficial.

For the time that any one subject occupied his mind, it was pursued with such whole-headed zeal and vigour and exhaustiveness, that *that one* seemed as if it must be *the pursuit* of his life.

He went deeply into the study of Natural Philosophy; and found it quite natural that he should compare his thoughts and their results with those of Sir Isaac Newton, where they met on musical grounds.

This penetrating and microscopic sense of his seemed to accompany and to govern him in all subjects that attracted him as being worthy of thought at all.

Such was his tone of mind when, quite young, he took up Chemistry, and then, later, Mechanics, and the abstruse Science of Acoustics, and the laws of the String, and the nature of Sound. What a fountain of glorious action and investigation is indicated by these flowing and unending streams of thought, going out, as it were, into so many lands and regions of inquiry !

Side by side with the universality of his inventiveness, goes his practicableness.   He always saw that he could gain his point, though he knew well the means to do so could be improved. Each one of his schemes meant something useful, something to help on to more perfect knowledge.   This is easy to see; and the only things difficult to realize as we read are his youth and *far-ahead-ativeness*, according to the advancement of art and science then, and the practical application of so many subjects on which he wrote and thought. Many of his plans and inventions may appear crude, but their very clearness and possibility disarm criticism, and we love to read them as the honest, ingenious workings of a solitary young thinker, seventy years ago.   He always had a clear purpose, a well-defined plan ; he knew what he wanted to do, and often solved difficult problems by the work of his own brain before he had recourse to help from other minds.

He seems to turn to his diary-friend under every stress of thought, every painful difficulty in life, every outward-run of inventive fancy, every passing feeling, whether sorrowful, hopeful, depressing, exhilarating, joyful, crushing, almost annihilating—so keen was his sensitiveness—as one by one, either in the newly awakened energy of the morning, the driving activities of the day, the reflection and sociality of the evening, or the sublime meditative solitude of midnight, they swept by turn the chords of that spirit-harp so truly called "A Harp of a thousand strings," so keenly responsive was its sound to the touch of their unseen hands.

We are surprised also as we read the exquisitely *written* book; not a dot, or a comma, or a word wanted or omitted.

It is wonderful also to observe how, after securing his Doctorate with all the labour and study and real work which his Exercise evinces, and which would have been to many a sufficient and whole life-work, he was still not content, but pursued with unabated vigour many other branches of science, in addition to the one in which he had gained pre-eminence. He seemed to revel in his dips into Acoustics and Sound, Harmonic Proportions, etc. His sign was ever upward; ever a learner, ever advancing.

Another thing I see as I read is *his face* over his book. He speaks of his having "real delight" in his thoughts and some results of his beautiful Harmonic experiments. How many have delicate sensibility of thought, of perception and knowledge to follow him there? I have seen his face brim over with happy thought as he realized his own suggestions. Indeed, I can describe his face on many occasions, but as one full of happy thought, and expressing a contented, intellectual goodness.

Reading at this late day of another, also unknown till gone from us, the following words, relating to *him*, come with great force applied to my Father: " A high and reverend simplicity, which vindicates the greatness of real goodness, and the goodness of real greatness."

His life teems with touching incidents and lofty thoughts which discover his great heart. His sympathy with those in sickness or in sorrow was sincere and practical, and instances of its generous and self-denying expression are without number. They glint and glisten on the structure of his beautiful character, as the sunlight tips and touches, point by point, the interior of one of our own cathedrals. Intelligence and benignity were the lights of his face and the manifestation of his spirit; but far more than any glowing eulogy would he prefer me to say what all who knew him believed to be true; the same words that he used of another during his Bristol life: " A more honest and upright man than he was, is perhaps not to be found on the surface of God's earth." True of himself also are his few words on the departure for Dublin of Dr. Okely, the Moravian minister, a man whom he loved and highly esteemed : " Thus has left us one of the greatest men Bristol ever knew ; nay, Bristol knew him not."

Two decades will soon have passed away since my Father " fell on sleep." For fully two-thirds of that time I could write nothing. If I attempted it, tears blurred the page as I realized that the rare and beautiful character I saw unfolded only too late to take it in, either as a whole or in detail, was gone from me forever.

By effort—continued effort—I made myself dwell on his earlier life, till it grew into an intense fascination. I lost sight of my Father in the beautiful and gifted young life I saw opening out before me. I felt for him so keenly in his struggles that I longed to have been there to aid and sympathize with him. I saw how the hard, practical duties to which he fell heir, clashed with, but never quenched his ambition and his determination to attain to the lofty position in art and usefulness, which by his natural gifts he knew to be his. I watched his fortitude and endurance in difficulty and trouble ; I marked his increasing diligence in the pursuit of knowledge, and the manifestations of his varied and versatile gifts. Passing on to his maturer life, it seemed as though his pages became luminous as he told simply of kindly deeds, and unselfish acts, and sympathy never withheld. Each glimpse of his many-sided character opened up other scenes as interesting to describe as the last. Both his works and his life are its illustration ; the latter a living example, his musical works an embodiment of scientific thought and consecration of talent, moving upwards to the unattainable here and the perfect knowledge hereafter.

I saw his great diligence for his children's sake, and as I realized what he had done for me, and what I owe him, I found that this only was left to me : To tell from my heart what would recall him to other hearts that loved him ; or, if I should not reach them, that those who knew him not " in the flesh " would, through my words, detect the great, kindly, human heart, and the excellent Christian spirit, which in him were mingled with the soul of the Church Musician, and which appeared in his daily walk, as well as in the loftiest strains of his ennobling harmony.

I could tell how he never feared that " enemy in the rear, wasted time " ; and that, without help of any kind to make him a scholar, he yet became a Scholar in the truest enlightenment of intellect and mind. I could show that although he received no help to make him a Musician, yet he became one of England's most learned sons in music; and further, that although he had no training in distinctive Church principles, yet he himself became not only a learned man in her theology, but an ornament to that branch of it which England claims as her own ; which is strengthened by the mighty intellects of her sons, and sealed by her martyrs' blood.   He would not despise my effort.   Indeed, many things he said to me when he had passed through and borne the burden and heat of the day and come to his eventide rest, and which I now recall, have been an incentive and spur to my action.

I also realized that while my Father's life was one of singular coherence and unity of aim, it had been a divided life—divided by an ocean—spent in two hemispheres.   And if it were impossible for me to collect the material for an account of that life as a whole, I could at least bridge the chasm, and give enough to satisfy friends on either shore until the fuller narrative shall appear, of the love and esteem in which he was held in his own old city, and of his remarkable experience and triumph at Cambridge ; and at the same time, tell to friends here of his work in Church Music in the New World ; of the love of true hearts there, and of the widespread influence he gained in his self-chosen

character of a " Musical Missionary " ; and also in
the more pathetic words he loved to adopt and apply
to himself, that he was but a " stranger and a sojourner in the land."

F. H. H.

LONDON, 1886.

EDWARD HODGES.

ALL SAINTS' AND ST. NICHOLAS' CHURCH, BRISTOL.

EDWARD HODGES.

CHAPTER I.

BOYHOOD AND YOUTH.

EDWARD HODGES was born in Bristol, that old commercial seaport, smoky city of churches and high chimneys, on the 20th of July, 1796. His father's residence, warehouses, and place of business were all in Bridge Street, near the Churches of St. Mary-le-Port and St. Nicholas, and not far from Bristol Bridge. It was not a very encouraging atmosphere for a scholar or an artist; yet here, in spite of all discouragements, the extraordinary gifts of which young Edward was the possessor, pushed their way into notice, as wind-sown plants will do in shady and stony nooks.

His early childhood marked him as possessing a delicate, intellectual, and sensitive nature; but he had a good constitution. His rudimental instruction in music, which was all the musical instruction

he ever received, ceased at the age of eleven
or twelve. Probably his school life did also. Of
that period no record remains ; but this tradition
exists, which comes from a source on which we are
bound to rely : " There is no mischief in the school,
but Ned Hodges is at the bottom of it." So said
the master.

His father, Archelaus Hodges, was the head of
a large paper business, and it was his wish, expressed
also in his will, that his son Edward, the eldest of
three brothers, should succeed to it.

The time came only too soon. His father, to
whom he was deeply and tenderly attached, died
when Edward was fifteen years old, and his mother
followed him two years afterwards. The home was
broken up and the little family scattered. The
brothers were sent to school, the sister was taken
by loving friends, and Edward went to live with his
cousin, Mr. W. H. Baily, the brother of the sculptor, E. H. Baily, R.A.

As the years in his regularly-kept diaries are now
seen to pass under his honest and graphic pen, we
have a marvellous unfolding of the leaves of a life.
We find him applying himself to the business as
steadily as a youth of life and vigour of mind could
do to work that was not only hard and without a
particle of pleasure, but which awakened absolute

dislike. His punctuality, integrity, good sense, honour, honesty, and general trustworthiness were all brought into play in turn ; and, young as he was, he was consulted and his opinion taken in all matters requiring judgment and discrimination. At the same time he was full of love for all active sports, especially boating and skating. At skating he was a great adept, and he invented and drew diagrams of the Rolling Skate. This is substantially the same as was invented later, and first used in Paris. This and two or three other inventions— one which he named a " Bundle Machine," to relieve the burden of raising heavy loads on to the backs of men, another for breaking large stones, and one for raising heavy ladders,—were only the first of the long list of inventions he recorded, some of the most important of which are hereafter mentioned.

His intellect was stimulated by wide and comprehensive reading. His gradually collected library contained works on Chemistry, Geometry, Theology, History, Poetry, Logic, Mathematics, Architecture, and Mechanical Science. Into Chemistry he went quite exhaustively. He spent all his money in books and chemical apparatus for experiments. Places of amusement are never even mentioned in his diary. He procured the best author-

ities on every subject. Of languages, Latin was
his favourite, and he used it for his daily journal for
months, in order to acquire fluency in it. He
studied German and French, and desired to add a
knowledge of Hebrew and Greek, but time did not
allow of their pursuit.

And where is Music all the while, the great
master-study of his life ? It seemed all these years
of his youth to be only a delightful social enjoyment and recreation. The earliest mention of his
playing is that, while still a child, his father is
reported to have often said to him, "Come, Ned,
play me 'Lord of all power and might.'" He was
very fond of practical jokes, and once puzzled his
father by shutting the cat in on the piano keys, and
sitting down to read, quite ignorant, apparently, as
to who was the player of the modern "Cat's
Fugue."

On the breaking up of the Bridge Street home a
sale was advertised of all the household effects, including the organ. My Father was distressed at the
idea of losing his beloved organ, and spoke to his
cousin, Mr. Baily, and found that he had a friend
at court. Mr. Baily, who was one of his father's
executors (the other one being in favour of selling
the organ), not only said that the organ should not
be sold, but that it must be brought to his house

that very night. Off went Edward in high glee. He had some delay and difficulty in securing the keys of the deserted house. That done, he got Samuel, his porter, another man, and a barrow, and before long they were pulling the organ all to pieces, placing it on the barrow, locking up the house, and wheeling away the dissected instrument through the dark streets to Mr. Baily's house in St. James's Square. The mysterious little procession arrived at the house, my young Father set hard to work, and by nine o'clock had it all put together again. He then had a good "play" on it to celebrate its arrival and the discomfiture of those who on the morrow would go to view the " Organ for sale."

In his early youth he and his intimate friends formed a Musical Society. They numbered eight or nine, and played both wind and stringed instrument. Money now went for violincello, violin, and tenor, all of which instruments my Father played, though the 'cello was his favourite. Their music was also an important item of expenditure : they bought largely, and of the works of the best composers, though they seem to have played chiefly Hook's and Haydn's Concertos. They also formed a Debating Society, and my Father studied and practised speaking, so as to be able to express himself in public thoughtfully and fluently.

Sunday attendance at the Bridge Street Independent Chapel, of which his father was a member, and later at Church, was never omitted, except in case of illness, through all these years. The sermons he heard directed his attention to intellectually-religious subjects, and of these he loved to converse. His religious opinions were matters of conviction ; he had fought his way to them without bias from any party either in the religious or secular world, and therefore he could help others, and he did. When his friends crossed the line between revelation and rationalism, he was distressed for them, and not only argued as one whose feet were firmly set on the " things which cannot be shaken," but by lending them scholarly books and bringing forward the power of his own educated reason, he strove with them to bring them back to the only sure line of thought. To him science and religion were inseparable.

My Father's earliest associations were not in the Church. His convictions and affections led him to it by a gradual process of thought, after the reading and study of many learned writers on the subject. His mind, by its very construction, could have rested nowhere else. His love, his loyalty, his artistic sense, could only have been satisfied in that Church of his own country, in whose glorious liturgy and services his highest gifts found utterance. During his early manhood he had an intense desire to study for Holy Orders, but the obstacles to the attainment of his hopes were too great to be overcome, and he was obliged reluctantly to abandon them.

His remarkable and almost sudden development of latent musical powers may have been due to his early concerted practice of music with his companions, and the pleasure they had in it; for afterwards, when writing full anthems without previous study, his accompaniments showed a knowledge both of orchestration and instrumentation. As he played his part in these early gatherings, one feels that he must have noted not only the musical structure and combination, but also the scope, the individuality, the nature, and powers of each instrument employed. As he listened and played, improvements suggested themselves, which he afterwards planned, in the trumpet, the trombone and the pianoforte; thus he proceeded step by step, from the power to render simply and musically the simplest melody, to the farthest intricacies of double counter-point and fugue.

CHAPTER II.

IT is the early Spring of 1818.   Leaving smoky old Bristol by chaise or coach, and passing through already green country, we arrive at the old Town of Malmesbury.

The River Avon runs through, and round about it; and we soon catch a glimpse of what remains of one of the largest, richest, and most ancient of the abbey foundations of England.   We pass the still perfect Market Cross; and through a Norman gateway we enter the ancient churchyard, thronged with monuments and tombstones, below which lies the human dust of many centuries.   We see the whole southern side of the Abbey Church before us.   The massive tower arches to the west; and parts of the walls of the transept to the eastern end, though broken, are still standing, half covered with rich thick ivy.   We see the beautiful Clere-story windows, the flying buttresses, and the rare stone tracery around the upper walls.   Only the nave is left; transept, choir, lady chapel, all are torn away and gone.

MALMESBURY ABBEY.

Let us enter this great Norman archway, a twin-sister to the one at Tewksbury Abbey. This is now the Parish church. Across the eastern end is a great modern, unsightly wall. What massive, noble columns are these! What would we not give for a sight of this Abbey Church at the time when, instead of the plastered wall, there opened to view the sombre glories of the eastern end! Passing up the aisle between the rigid, grand columns, is a group of a few persons. They pass up to the altar rail. It is a wedding : the bridegroom is the young Bristol musician, Edward Hodges ; the bride, Miss Margaret Robertson.

Miss Margaret Robertson was the youngest daughter of Mr. Matthew R. H. Robertson, of Maunditts Park, Malmesbury, Wilts. Her family were Moravians, *i.e.*, members of Count Zinzendorf's order of the Grain of Mustard Seed, also named the " Unitas Fratrum." She was educated at the Moravian school at Tytherton, renowned for its high standard of music. In this art, Margaret distinguished herself, and became a thorough student. She understood Harmony and Modulation, and was able to take my Father's duty at the organ if he were prevented by sickness. But it was in vocal music that her rare excellence lay. Her voice was one of power and exceeding sweetness.

She rendered the solos of Handel and Haydn with superb effect, and especially revelled in that grand free air by Handel, "O had I Jubal's lyre, and Miriam's tuneful voice." This she sang at St. Nicholas's Church, Bristol, at the baptism of her second son, Jubal, to whom it seemed natural that she should transmit a magnificent organ talent, as she transmitted her tuneful voice to her daughter Miriam, who as a child possessed a wonderful voice in compass and sweetness.

My Father records his resolution to choose none but a musical wife. She was united to him on the day she was nineteen. A romp in childhood, she grew up to be a happy-hearted, winning, amiable, lovely girl; and developed into a devoted, loving wife and mother. She bore the affliction of a long illness without a murmur, and even cheerfully. And as my memory holds her dear, she was one in whom, during her short life here below, dwelt every Christian grace.

The Children of Edward and Margaret Hodges were:

	DIED AT THE AGE OF
George Frederick Handel	20 years.
Faustina Hasse . .	72 years.
Miriam . . .	15 years.
Jubal	42 years.
John Sebastian Bach . .	
Deborah	2 years (about)
Cecilia	1 year (about)
Asaph	

Not long did my Father remain in the dull and noisy surroundings of the Bridge Street parental home where he took his bride in 1818. He found his way naturally enough towards the Cathedral. Passing through the Norman gateway, which no doubt was the principal entrance to the Monastery of St. Augustine, he came to an irregular building in the Lower Green, called the Prior's Lodge. This was the only picturesque and interesting relic of old times left. It at once arrested his attention, and he swiftly saw what, with a little time and money, he could make of it. It was Canon Ridley's house for two months in each year, when "in residence," while my Father could occupy it during the other ten months. So, as he used to say, "he commenced operations."

The change that came over the old building in a few months was marvellous. In the great gable, looking westward, he put a large Gothic stained-glass church window; and here was his capacious music room. The outside was imposing, the inside arranged for music. On the apex of the gable, he put a stone cross, and up to it before long the ivy climbed. He planted many trees, and himself cultivated his sequestered garden, trained and pruned his vines, and gathered grapes plentifully,—chiefly, as he says, " for Margaret."

The London *Athenæum* thus refers to Priory Lodge shortly after its demolition in 1884 :

" The fine old fifteenth century house at the S. W. angle of the Bristol Cathedral, the so-called ' Minster House' or 'Prior's Lodge,' has recently been pulled down, quite without excuse, by the Dean and Chapter. It was not only a valuable specimen of Mediæval architecture, but was also of special value as being one of the very small parts that still existed of the monastic buildings of the old Augustine Abbey of Bristol."

Here in Priory Lodge his amateur musical friends regularly assembled in numbers, enjoying to the utmost his social gatherings, and singing his newly-composed anthems, and anon the catches and glees which his humorous and fertile fancy threw off with ease and freedom. " Truly," he said, " my music room is the envy of one sex and the admiration of the other." It was indeed altogether a dwelling that would satisfy the most ecclesiastical craving, being, as it were, under the very shadow of the Cathedral Tower.

We get little pictures at this time of his musical life in the Prior's Lodge very pleasant to see. I make a few Diary extracts, including his words written on the day of his taking possession :

" Sept. 27, 1822. Hard at it in removing. Struck the

bedsteads and fairly changed my habitation. Dined at Bridge St. for the last (regular) time, and after much bustle and some little confusion, we all had comfortable tea here in College Green. May the LORD preserve us and make us to show forth His praise here tenfold more than we ever have done in our former house.

"N. B. At midnight I was in my Oriel window enjoying the beauties of the look-out by *moonlight*.

"Oct. 5. Immediately after breakfast, I proceeded to business and labouring hard all day I got the Organ together and in tolerable tune before 9 o'clock. I then sang a Solo ('Now Vanish') from the Creation. The music goes capitally in that new room; but I *must* get a new Organ.

"Oct. 12. My brother Britton popped in to supper, and we had a little music; he with his Flute, Margaret the Organ, and I the second Violin or Tenor.

"Dec. 9. We had some Instrumental Music, I playing second Violin! Margaret the Organ, Kimber, Bass; Hill, Flute; Withington, 1st Violin.

"26. William Okely and I amused ourselves by scraping on the Fiddle and Bass. Went skating again with Okely.

"I have given one grand Rout at which one of the Sheriffs of the City did me the honour to be present."

In numbering his household at the end of the year he says:

"Myself as Master
Margaret as Mistress
G. F. H. H., a son and heir
Two maids
Nimrod the dog, and
The cat, whom we brought from Bridge St., and who seems to relish her new quarters very much.

From my little Study in the Lower College Green."

"Jan. 9, 1823. In the evening Daniell came, and he Margaret and I played some hour or two on the Flute, Violin and Piano!!! Prior to that Margaret and I played through a whole volume of Duetts (viz. Don Juan by Dr. Crotch) on the grand Piano.

"June 15. Spent two hours at Howell's playing Sonatas at sight with Violin and Bass accompaniment. I was nearly all the morning practising Bach.

"19. At the Cathedral; sang Bass through the whole service."

"July 2. Tuned the old Harpsichord for little Crook's practice." Previously he says, "I occupied myself the whole morning in doctoring the old Harpsichord." And again, "I accompanied Mr. Hague on his Violin in some ancient music on my Harpsichord, in true antique style."

My Father gave a succession of concerts in his Music room, which he styled the " Nailheart Concerts." They were largely attended; on one occasion seventy and upwards, who all went away highly pleased with their entertainment, a good supper always following the music. Sometimes he calls these parties "Grand Bawls." They seemed to have been mightily enjoyed, the singers and performers being amateurs and friends. They also had a society called "The Larks." They met at 7 A.M., and sang an hour before breakfast. My Father says, on one occasion, "I composed a Catch for my morning company the day before."

On referring to the list of his compositions, we see that this year he had the heaviest musical works on hand, and was not only doing the duty of two Churches and superintending the erection of Clifton Organ, but composing services and anthems for particular occasions in the Church. I omit many entries of his practice at the organ of the fugues of Bach and the overtures by Handel. Of the former, on a previous occasion, he writes: "In the evening I had an hour or two's spell out of Sebastian Bach. His noble fugues are an inexhaustible source of delight."

The organ of St. James's was opened on Sunday, May 2d, 1824, and was the first in England having the C Compass, and 32 ft. pipe.

Diary. May 1, 1824. Prior's Lodge.
"The music went off well, and for the greater part of the time I felt in good spirits for the performance."

"May 3d. I was almost all day receiving the gratulations of my friends on our yesterday's exhibition, which seems to have given universal satisfaction.

"May 7th. I received a letter from the Vestry Clerk enclosing the thanks of the Vestry of St. James's for my complex exertions and a vote for a Snuff Box.

"This is as it should be. What shall I do next?"

"17. Margaret and I played through a long duett of Beethoven. In the evening I practised on the Piano-forte and Harpsichord, Moscheles, Bach and Scarlatti.

"June 20. I attended the Organ Committee Meeting, where I was presented in due form with my GOLD SNUFF BOX.

"Withington informed me that the Right Worshipful the Mayor intends filling my new box with snuff for me."

A Bristol paper, subsequently to 1850, speaks thus of St. James's Church and organ :

" The Benedictine Priory and Parish Church of St. James's, Barton, were built in 1129 ; the tower in 1374.   The Church is one of the oldest structures in Bristol, the nave being Norman.

" The celebrated Dr. Hodges was once organist here.

" The Western Gallery contains the largest organ in Bristol, having four rows of keys.   This Organ is a re-construction (in 1824) under the direction of Dr. Hodges.   Besides being the first in England to have the 32 feet C, and most of the Doctor's improvements, it has his own Triple Slat swell of tremendous *crescendo* power, from the veriest *pianissimo*.

" The tower has a ring of ten bells of remarkable beauty of tone.

" The motto on the fifth (B) is, ' FEAR GOD and honour the king.' "

In September, 1824, he removed from the Prior's Lodge to the Prebendal House in the Cloisters, belonging to Lord William Somerset, Canon of the Cathedral.

Of the Bristol Cloister properly speaking (*i.e.*, the arcade of stone-work which formerly lined each

side of the quadrangle, as at Gloucester and West-
minster now) only the eastern side remains.   This
has entrances to the Cathedral, the Chapter Room,
the Churchyard, and the Bishop's Palace.   These
cloisters surrounded the burial grounds of the
monks in many cathedrals; though some of them
may have been done away with in the destructive
changes that overtook our monastic establishments
in the reign of Henry VIII.

Within this Bristol Cloister one of the grandest
specimens of Norman architecture is to be found,
consisting of the vestibule of the Chapter Room,
and the Chapter Room itself; the interlaced arches
being in perfect preservation, and the pillars of the
vestibule very massive and grand.   My Father's
residence occupied the whole southern side of the
quadrangle.   There was something fascinating to
him in all this, and here he used to walk and medi-
tate at night, when no sound broke the stillness but
the watchman's rather plaintive cry, and the regular
sound of the Cathedral quarter-bell.

It is probable that he here thought out his degree
exercise ; his chosen words being "The dead praise
not Thee, O LORD, neither all they that go down
into silence."   At that time as he may have stood
at the churchyard gate when the night wind swept
coldly over the thickly-laid graves, the words would

come with terrible meaning, but he follows them with the succeeding words of life and action : " But we will praise the LORD from this time forth for evermore.   Praise the LORD."

There was in my Father a blending of the contemplative—and even a strong vein of the sentimental —with an intensely practical nature ; that ability to *work* which even Goethe seems to think but another name for genius.   It may be that this union of the sublime in thought with the intensely practical in work forms the true artist.

Here then in the cloisters my Father made his home during the remainder of his Bristol life.

He continued his work at composition, including many settings of whole Psalms, and his Coronation Anthem, with full orchestral accompaniments, for King William IV. This latter he considered one of his best works.   The rambling house, museum-like in appearance, resounded with the sound of these anthems, grandly rendered by the large musical parties assembled there : my young mother, and afterwards my brother Handel, who inherited her vocal talent, always sustaining the leading parts.

My Father also had frequent chess parties, being exceedingly fond of the game. His social circle increased rapidly and steadily, and being fearful that the frequent informal gatherings would inter-

fere with his work and home regularity, he put up the following couplet :

" All those who wish to be welcome again,
  Must please to move homeward at half past ten."

His visits to the Philosophical and Commercial Rooms brought him into contact with all the scientific men of the neighbourhood. His knowledge in Mechanical Science was said to be profound, and his suggestions and plans always in advance of his time.

As a citizen of Bristol his influence became widely felt. He was identified with her progress in every way. He was consulted on public questions, and his presence was sought on civic occasions. Whether at public dinner or meeting, the impression he left on the minds of all with whom he was associated was one of splendid moral courage, unflinching principle, clear common sense and foresight, and perfect courtesy as a gentleman. In politics he was a Tory ; but his great heart was liberal. Strong in his churchmanship, his Christianity was broad as God's light.

His prolific pen also brought him into notice in many political scenes ; one of his poems, published in the *Mirror*, entitled " Scenes in a Town Council," which I produce here, was full of strength, satire, and humour.

SCENES IN A TOWN COUNCIL.

I.

I have seen on a fine summer's morn
The industrious ants at their toil;
How they labour, a small grain of corn
To warehouse beneath the hard soil.

II.

I have witnessed the bees at their work
Exploring the blossoms all o'er;
How they filch every sweet that may lurk
Within them to add to their store.

III.

These things, I have seen with delight
And would witness with pleasure again;
But alas! what a different sight
When I turn to the doings of men!

IV.

The ants and the bees,
Though they forfeit their ease,
No doubt *their own pleasure* pursue;
And in this one respect
'Tis not hard to detect
A resemblance to that which *men* do.

V.

But if you ask to what that pleasure tends,
Then here, alas! the pretty likeness ends,
    For bees and ants
    (Like trees and plants)
Subserve the purpose of their first formation,

> But who will dare
> The same declare
> Of this perverse, vain-boasting generation.

VI.

> Such was the salutation of the Muse
> When recently she came,
> After long absence, to inquire the news
> Of the Town-Council game.
>> Etc., etc.

In the spring of 1829 the " No Popery " agitation took place, and Bristol was much excited in consequence of Mr. Peel's bill for the admission of Roman Catholics to seats in Parliament. Swiftly my Father's spirit moved as this breeze swept over the land, and February 8th the following spirited poem, written partly on Sunday in his organ gallery during service at St. James's Church, was produced. By Tuesday it was printed and posted up in the city. His diary says :

"My poem seems to attract public attention very strongly."

The next day he set it to music as solo and chorus ; "aiming at simplicity and truth more than learning," and sent it up to London for immediate publication.

No doubt he mingled with the crowds on the Exchange who stood there reading his spirited

patriotic words ; few, if any, of them knowing that
the quaint, pleasant, thoughtful-looking young man,
with the broad-brimmed hat and unfashionable cut
of coat, was the author of them.

NO POPERY.

Up men ! for your Country, your Altars, your King,
And this be the cry with which Heav'n's vault shall ring,
                    No Popery.

Though Ministers flinch and the Premier turn tail,
The Protestant spirit shall ever prevail.
Then rouse yourselves, Britons, bestir you like men ;
Your lives may be *once* lost, but never again.
        Up then for your Country, etc.

Be courage, and firmness and wisdom combined—
And charity too, in each Protestant mind ;
But let not the *march of concession* o'erwhelm
The Protestant safeguards of Britain's fair realm.
        Up then for your Country, etc.

Our fathers where are they ? Some, led to the stake
For conscience, for faith, and for liberty's sake,
Were fearfully martyred by Rome's cruel men,
Whose creed is *the same at this day* as 't was then.
        Up then for your Country, etc.

The right both of Papists and Turks we admit,
To worship their Maker as they may see fit ;
And yet, not contented with this, they demand
A right to make Laws for our Protestant land.
        Up then for your Country, etc.

Now God save our King, our Religion, and Laws,
And help us if need be to die for our cause ;
Our famed Constitution preserved unimpaired
May thus by our childrens' descendants be shared.

Up then ! for your Country, your Altars, your King,
And this be the cry with which Heav'n's vault shall ring,
                              No Popery.

As a child I was often taken by my mother to St. James's Church on a Sunday evening.

I remember the sound of the bells as we walked up that churchyard which was so terribly filled with grave-stones. I remember the sight of the crowds in the galleries under the Norman arches and below, as we passed up the narrow stair to the organ : and the glance into my Father's mysterious little organ-box as I passed the door,—truly a magician's den to me.

Then from my little corner by the green curtain, I could watch him as he sat before his four ranks of keys. The organ-loft was roomy, divided by the projecting choir-organ as usual. I used to listen for the sound my Father made in drawing his stops ; and catch his animated glances as he spoke to the gentlemen opposite, or to his beautiful son Handel, who stood at a raised desk at his left. There was such an air of power and mystery about my Father as his face and form were brought out

into relief by the gloom of his organ-box behind
him. And what a change would come over his
face as he began to play! " Play " is not the word.
There was both in his face and in the sounds he
evoked from the keys and the pipes around him, a
suggestion of something unearthly, almost indescribable.

It was customary at St. James's to sing the
hymn

" From all that dwell below the skies "

before the service, without its being " given out."
So it fell to my Father's lot to announce the entrance of the clergy, and to bring the whole mass
of the great congregation to their feet : and this he
did magnificently, at the same time raising, by his
magic power, the immense volume of singing from
below, which was like the surging of the sea. I
gazed down on the great crowd, the many lights
seeming only to render the old Norman building more sombre as they revealed the crowded
galleries and recesses behind the round arches and
heavy columns, and the great dim painting of the
Transfiguration covering the eastern wall of the
church. Both the sight and the sound were overpowering to me. I felt that my Father was not
playing ; it was a wonderful spiritual giving out of

himself into his music,—or I should say, into the grand words his music carried to every heart. It absolutely controlled the hundreds below, drew out their voices at his will, and sent an electric thrill through all. " Eternal are Thy mercies, Lord ! " Mercy reaching to endless ages was the " eternal truth " he made us feel.

> " His praise shall sound from shore to shore,
>   Till suns shall rise and set no more."

This was the climax, which he, with illuminated countenance and magnetic force, *made* us feel.

He did not merely play ; he forced on us great religious truths. He played on spirits, not on keys only ; and through the stops of his organ he unstopped our ears to voices not of this world.

It was then, as he brought out the words of Eternal Truth, that I *first saw my Father's face.* It was a vision of an inspired and transformed countenance. Its light was a living one, spiritual and inward, and gleamed with an intense happiness, as, revelling in the consciousness of his own powers, his spirit seemed to ride those rolling waves of harmony which he evoked from his magnificent organ. I cannot describe it ; it was the face of a spiritual conqueror ; and I know that what I saw in it then is that by which I shall know him hereafter.

Very original was my Father's way of summoning us to his study to give us our lesson in singing the scale.

Opening his door, he began to "tune up his fiddles," on the piano, which was our call. It was an improvization in imitation of tuning the orchestra to the dominating A, with its background of harmony.

Running from any occupation or any part of the house, we made for the study, and took our places around him at his right, according to our ages, and listened. From the leading A came the E (fifth) above, his fingers purposely stumbling on the E♭ as though it needed tuning up—the other string notes, the fifths below, followed ; while all the while he ran freely on in all possible modulations, his organ-chords grandly rolling in, and the penetrating, persistent A always steadily there, till at length, with his countenance lighted up with pleasure, he got his fiddles all tuned up, and made a grand finale, while we stood watching, listening, and taking in the scene in silence.

He then proceeded to give a lesson in *the scale*, and in holding long notes, and managing our breath. He paid great attention to crescendo and diminuendo, and always took us to the easy extent of our voices, avoiding straining them. He taught us how to *breathe in* and *retain* breath, as I, many years after, watched Jenny Lind do.

If any one of us did not open his mouth sufficiently, a gag was threatened and applied.

These were lessons of great value for life, both in harmony and modulation, and in the true principles of vocalization ; and never afterwards could I attend a concert and listen to the tuning of the orchestra and hear the fifths crowding in, in their musical confusion, while the organ behind them—that great thing of solid and overwhelming power—was reducing them to order and compelling them to agreement, without being carried back to that far-off old cloister study, and seeing again my Father's playful, kindly, and beaming face, as, with the serried ranks of books beyond him, he sat at his piano, backing with such spirited and manifold harmonies the ever-recurring, irresistible A.

After a good practice in many keys he "chaunted" the "*Nunc Dimittis*" with us, and the lesson was done.

CHAPTER III.

IN May, 1825, at the age of twenty-eight, my Father entered Sydney Sussex College, Cambridge, as a Fellow Commoner, and proceeded to his Doctorate there, without taking the degree of Bachelor previously, as is usual. In this he was strenuously opposed by Dr. Clark-Whitfield, Professor of Music at Cambridge, and organist of Hereford Cathedral. The Professor also advised him to go to Oxford for his degree. This aroused the spirit of the sister university, and an effort was immediately made to get him entered at Trinity College. This was refused on the ground that no musical degree was there given. Of the correspondence which ensued between the Professor, my Father, and the Rev. Dr. Guildford Waite, of St. John's College, an old and valued friend of my Father's writes :

" Strange and almost incredible as it may appear, the young Bristol organist and musician, without

SIDNEY SUSSEX COLLEGE, CAMBRIDGE.

the culture and polish of a University course, stands out unmistakably superior, not only in the clear-cut sufficiency of his flawless English, but in ready, yet elegant, mastery of a perfect epistolary style. He never loses his imperturbable patience ; his temper remains cool and collected ; he is never betrayed into the natural and even justifiable pungency of a disputant who carries the most precious interests of his career in his hand. The letters of Mr. Hodges exhibit a world of practical shrewdness, foresight, and the quiet assurance of one who is confident of success and victory. The key to the story of his success is found in the lively personal interest that Dr. Waite had conceived in the brilliant reputation which Mr. Hodges had already achieved, which had long outgrown the critical and æsthetic appreciation of his provincial city.

" Although a cathedral city, that reputation had failed of recognition among the old-time officials and place-holders. The simple fact that Mr. Hodges had presumed upon a career of the highest ecclesiastical music without the indispensable pupilage at the feet of a cathedral organist—and if we may trust the testimony of contemporaries, not a few of the cathedral organists were poorly qualified for their high vocation,—settled the question so far as Mr. Hodges was concerned, at least among the cathedral officials of Bristol, and he was turned over to a larger, nobler criticism outside.

" Dr. Waite proved to be the man needed at that pivotal period. Without his energetic, almost impetuous urgency, and his semi-official representation, the young musician would not, then at least, have recognized the narrowness of his environment, and demanded a more authoritative and learned recognition.

" The world has changed since 1825, even in Cambridge. It is an altogether different world that awaits the aspirant for honors in the musical profession now. Nothing seems left to accident or conjecture ; everything is anticipated and provided for.

" A resident Professor of Music represents the University, and promotes rather than obstructs the operations of the statutes. Procedure is amply marked out, and no man worthy to enter into the examinations is left at loss or in doubt. No nook or cranny remains for lurking prejudice or personal animosities. There are the statutes, there the procedure, and there the examination papers, read and known of all men concerned. The result is absolutely determined by the candidate himself. If he succeeds in " flooring " his several " papers " within the required conditions, his degree is sure. Indeed, it appears that the conditions are quite as generous towards the candidate as they are just to the integrity of the University.

" How differently circumstances shaped themselves in 1825!

" The road to the acquisition of the musical doctorate had almost ceased to be an open thoroughfare ; and only at rare intervals do we find records of one who had successfully braved its difficulties. The department of music itself, under such adverse conditions, had fallen far below its earlier renown, and the University, as represented by its legislative body, the Senate, had not only lost all interest in its operations, but had seriously considered the question of refusing it place or recognition among the University Faculties.   Even the proposition of abrogating the professorship was seriously considered ; the professor had, as a non-resident, practically withdrawn from university life ; and we find this extraordinary situation in the ancient University, that had for many generations conferred its doctorate upon many illustrious ones among Anglican composers, that for the time being it was without a musical Faculty, and more than indifferent to the culture of the divine art.

" It is hardly possible to repress a smile as we contemplate the Professor while opening *the exercise* sent up by the young aspirant.   Having at the out-

set laid down (or suggested) a four-part composition, while insisting on the preliminary Bachelor's
Degree, and afterwards waiving it under the com-
pulsion of the situation, for an exercise in eight parts,
he opens his eyes upon a composition in twelve
parts, duly orchestrated, abounding in consummate
graces and contrapuntal intricacies, in wealth and
dignity of invention, in fugue and canon, with
masterly treatment of three choirs, such as Purcell
would have admired, and even Handel might have
approved ! Here was a work, an *Opus* indeed, far
transcending the measure of his own artistic
capacity, while demonstrating the futility of his own
obstructive policy. He had assuredly never looked
upon such a masterpiece before from one seeking
University honors ; and we are left to wonder at
the maturity, fertility, and inspiration of a genius,
so modestly reared in the twilight, and reaching
such an exalted climacteric without the intervention
of masters, or schools ; the outgrowth of his own
untiring industry and recondite study.

"In comparison with this exercise for three choirs
in twelve parts, what superficial and even meretricious compositions, before and since that day, must
have bridged the way to a Doctor's degree, not only
in Cambridge but elsewhere !

"It is no longer *Ad Cantab*, but *In Cantab.*

TRINITY CHAPEL, CAMBRIDGE.

There is the eventful coaching journey along the most exquisite highways and byways, every mile of it rich in ancient and mediæval historic legend and association, and the young neophyte reaches the city of his pilgrimage.

" His alacrity and courage are wonderful. Nothing intimidates, hinders, or irritates him. He marshalls his forces, who promptly come from Bristol, London, Ely, etc. (for a consideration !), to see him through. Chapters in his diary fairly crackle and snap with brisk and crowded details that must be looked after. And in such a whirl of unwonted toil and excitement, this delicate, sensitive, highly-strung young man is, day after day, pushing his way towards the approaching crucial service on that Sunday in Great St. Mary's and the ceremonial to follow in the Senate House. He finds opportunity, through his growing celebrity, to give the University men and the public a taste of his quality at the keyboard of more than one college chapel organ, though the local organists are chary of any perilous competition. Then the perpetual demand for heavy fees, stipulated and provided for at the multiplied stages of his advance towards the Senate House ; they spring up at the most unlooked-for times. What a touch of nature is this, when he first assumes the college cap and gown and feels as if he had ' always been a gownsman ! '

" The evolution of order and even an approxima-
tion to an impressive delivery of his ' Exercise,'
seems something among the impossibilities.　Then
there is dramatic, almost tragic, interest in the story
of his buffeting and struggling in the crowd, which
beleaguered the doorway of St. Mary's, and nearly
crushed the life out of the slender composer before
he could reach the organ !　That the Exercise
' went off well ' after such an ordeal, is most
astonishing of all.

" It is only the sure, masterful hand that can pluck
success from the most hostile conjunction of circumstances, and that day assuredly the intrepid
young composer from Bristol had conquered, and
won his degree almost by acclamation."

His degree exercise was an anthem, in twelve
parts, for three choirs, chorus, orchestra, and organ.
The words were taken from the 17th and 18th
verses of the 115th Psalm : " The dead praise not
the Lord, neither any that go down into silence.
But we will bless the Lord, from this time forth
and for evermore.　Praise the Lord."　This anthem
was performed in the University Church of St.
Mary, Cambridge, on Sunday, the 3rd July, 1825,
with sixty-nine performers, before the Vice-Chancel-
lor of the University and the college dons, and a
very large congregation of undergraduates and

others ; and on the following Tuesday, my Father graduated as Bachelor and Doctor in Music, by accumulation, the ceremony taking place in the Senate House, Cambridge.

Apropos of the obstacles put in my Father's way towards taking his degree in music, I must quote from the able article or critique which appeared in the *London Quarterly Musical Magazine* on his " Morning and Evening Service and Two Anthems," published by D'Almaine & Co. in the same year, 1825.

The writer had been speaking of music in its highest sense, or rather what he terms the sublime in music, and says :

" When a composer therefore enters on this distinct and supreme department of his Art, he does well, be his talents what they may, provided his motives are as pure as human motives can be. The requisites for excellence in this exalted course are indeed limited to the gifted few ; for how few are great in genius, great in science, great in meditation ; but yet a sufficiency of science, with musical feeling, sincerity and piety, is no uncommon attainment, we hope ; and which he that possesses need not despair of exerting effectively on this elevated ground of mental exertion. That the world ever has duly appreciated, or ever will appreciate the highest objects of Music, let no man hope till knowledge, experience, fine feeling and reflection become common properties. Superior minds must be content to disseminate those principles of improvement in science and in virtue that may imperceptibly carry on the work of human reformation by the gradual advance of irresistible accumulation.

"When the principles of Music become generally understood, the art will be properly estimated, even by the many; and this knowledge is even now working its way silently, surely, and effectually amidst the frivolities of fashion and the choke-damp of professional competition.

"The last mentioned obstacle to struggling merit and popular improvement is a case in point of which our readers in general are undoubtedly not aware, unless the reports that have reached us are groundless; for a little bird sings, that much opposition has been made to granting the composer of the music before us his Diploma, though on what score we are at a loss to guess. Not on the score before us, we hope; which in our opinion qualifies the composer for the Degree as much as any exercise ever submitted to the Professor of Music at either of our Universities.

"Truly, we see no just cause or impediment why Dr. Hodges and Alma Mater should not be joined together, particularly after certain alliances of the kind we wot of, alliances as *outré* as that of the Doge of Venice to the Adriatic. '*De non apparentibus et non existentibus eadem est ratio.*'

"No such objections therefore occurring to us, we would fain ask in legal phraseology. 'If not, why not?'

"He that is ambitious to ascend this high scale of composition must qualify himself for the task by sufficiently studying the Cathedral music of our country, and this qualification Dr. Hodges possesses, in our humble opinion, as manifestly as any composer we know of, dead or alive.

"In a word, the publication before us, is a satisfactory proof that the Doctor has done that for which he is fully competent, and merits all the encouragement that such labours ever deserve, but seldom elicit."

From the Rev. W. H. Havergal to Dr. Hodges, December, 1825 :

"I know not whether to sympathize with you or congratulate you upon the ill and invidious treatment which it seems you are accustomed to meet with from the world. Perhaps it is fit I should do both. I am sure that I cordially feel for you, especially as your statements are novel to me. I had heard but little in a recent letter, and that little was manifestly the offspring of envy. Your answers to my queries will suit my purpose excellently well, and enable me to say exactly what I wish to say. But I must congratulate you. All this malice, and envy and calumny, and everything like mean and petty attempt to thwart you and depreciate you, only furnish to every candid and contemplative mind, a pretty urgent proof, that your rivals (if I may use that appellation) are conscious that they have somewhat to fear from you. Besides, this thorny path is the very road in which many an individual has proceeded to eminence. Did not Handel himself meet with much jealousy and vexation at his outstep in the world? I think he did ; but I have not time to refer ; you doubtless know whether he did or not. I can only say, *Do not* be discouraged. *Nil desperandum.* Abide by your motto. Practically too, mark and study your other signet. *Oremus* prepares the way for *Cantemus*, or still using ecclesiastical Latin, *Exultemus*. You know as well as I can remind you the exhortation which saith 'Commit thy way unto the LORD, and He shall bring it to pass.' 'Casting *all* your care, temporal as well as spiritual, on Him for He careth for you.'

"I do not know Dr. Crotch sufficiently to communicate with him ; I have spoken to him and that is all. I will most readily do anything that is within the compass

of my little power to forward your views. I shall try
hard to get your music into use at Canterbury. When
you are Editor of the *Musical Review* I shall take it in.
All I know of the Royal Institution is, that Dr. Crotch
gave up his good situation at Oxford for it."

On July 5, 1825, Mr. Havergal wrote :

" Woodcock, Organist of New College, Oxon, died
very recently. In his stead was elected a very young
man named Bennet. Merit only was the ground of his
appointment. Cross, Organist of St. John's College,
Christ Church, and the University, is also just dead. I
hear that the Dean and Chapter intend giving the situation to the most likely candidate. How glad should I
be to see you in a station of such eminence and opportunity ! Take the hint.

" W. H. H."

C. C. Clarke, Esq., to the Rev. W. H. Havergal :

" The Doctor's abilities certainly deserve a fair field for
their exercise.

" How his old opponent Cummins could think him
unworthy of a Degree surprises me ; for I believe a certain knowledge of the science qualifies for that—does it
not ? And *that* no one can dispute the Doctor possesses,
who knows anything at all about the matter. His possessing the power to create new musical ideas that shall be
pleasing to Mr. Cummins, or to any one else, is quite
another affair ; and in my mind would in no way affect
his reputation as a man of talent—though it would as a
man of genius.

" He is no ordinary man in either point of view.

" Believe me,

" Faithfully yours,

" C. C. CLARKE,

" Organist of Worcester Cathedral."

KING'S COLLEGE CHAPEL, CAMBRIDGE.

It is a source of pleasure to me to recall and revive these early years of my Father's friendship for Mr. Havergal. It was as strong as it was deep, and a very loving one; it began when they were both young men, my Father but twenty-eight, and Mr. Havergal three years older, and it lasted to the end of their lives.

There was something strongly akin in their souls; both having devoted their lives to the service of the Church. The one from the pulpit and desk sought help from the sacred musician at the organ, who he knew had devoted every intellectual power and the zeal of his life to the same sacred cause. This zeal did not pass in spasmodic effort, but continued after my Father had crossed the Atlantic.

From expressions in the letters we see that my Father had much to bear from the remarks of envious or jealous minds; and how much harder would it have been but for the strong help of this true and faithful friend. It was truly a brotherly love which existed between them; and it lasted till they, within but a year or two of each other, entered into that larger life beyond our ken, where, even now, they may not be divided.

I record here my own esteem for him and his loving wife, and my friendship for the bright and beautiful sacred minstrel, Frances Ridley Havergal, that subtle player on invisible harp-strings; for his other highly gifted daughters, and for my kind friend the late Francis T. Havergal, D.D., Prebendary of Hereford Cathedral.

CHAPTER IV.

IN 1821, as the year is just closing, my Father
writes :

"May God give me *faithfulness to myself* while I write
my Memorabilia," (as the Moravians have it).

" Music is, must be, and shall be my forte.   Here will I
dwell, for I have desired it : and even in Eternity it shall
accompany my joys and heighten Celestial bliss.   I have
dedicated it to the service of God : and trust He will add
His blessing upon my endeavours."

"I beseech Him, notwithstanding Mr. Biddulph's
anathema on 'Intellectual Attainments,' to grant me a
capacious intellect, and opportunity for constant progression in improvement; that I may grow in grace and in
the knowledge (He knows all things) of our Lord Jesus
Christ, to Whom be glory for ever.   Amen."

Diary Extract.

" July 27, 1825.

" Resolving not to waste more time, I commenced a
series of notes for Lectures or Essays on Music.

" I fear my knowledge of the subject is very confined,
but by a little labour perhaps I can brush up more.

" I apprehend the Theory of *Sound* itself, the basis of Music, is as yet very imperfect. At all events, be I where I may, I must do something. I think of cutting out my time into portions and devoting it to various studies. Among them, I must revive my lost Latin. I ought to get acquainted with Greek ; German and Italian are indispensable, as is also a knowledge of some branches of Mathematics. These things, coupled with the constant practice and composition of music, will find me plenty of employment."

" Aug. 15, 1825.

"Zinc Organ Pipes.

"I went with Charles Murray, Esq., to the manufactory of *Patent Zinc*, and took Smith, the Organ builder, with me. The object of my visit was to see whether that metal might not be made available in the construction of Organ pipes. I have hopes of it. *When warmed* it is easily bended to any shape, and, on cooling, fixes quite hard. It seems remarkably firm in its texture, and to have a sonorous quality. As left by the rolling mills too, its surface is remarkably smooth, a circumstance which I think of great importance for the interior of a pipe. They promised me to send a sheet of the metal to Smith's shop to try the experiment."

" Aug. 16, 1825.

" Mathematics.

" This morning before breakfast I professedly took my first lesson in mathematics. For this purpose Mr. T. S. Davies attended. It was rather a conversation than a lesson. Davies seemed to be a shrewd man and to have the 'root' (query Square root ?) of the matter in him. I am afraid my advances will be but slow. Sometimes I

fancy that my power of apprehension or comprehension
is not so quick as it once was. At other times I lose by its
rapidity. I understand a point perfectly and so pass on
before it has time to fix itself in my memory. . The next
day I have to refer to my first principle again. Davies
tells me that in order to cure myself of this propensity,
I must *work* several of the problems."

" Davies breakfasted with us. I lent him old Bishop
Wilkins' Philosophical and Mathematical works. In town
I fell in with Jackson the Artist. I met George Wash-
bourne, Master of St. Peter's Hospital, and he accompanied me to Smith's shop to enquire about the Zinc pipe
manufactory. Smith promised to make the experiment
next week. We all then went to St. Thomas's Church,
where Smith has been putting in two Copula movements,
and otherwise repairing the organ. I must again declare
I do not like the intrument. Although the tones are
good and the Church favourable to musical effect, the deficiency in the Bass of the instrument more than counter-
balances these advantages. Its having what is technically
called ' short octaves,' cripples all power of modulation.
The organ has no effect out of one or two keys.

" I played there for an hour, nearly, and then made
haste home."

" 1 March, 1826.

" It appears that my mind is now going to take a new
turn, as I feel a composing fit coming on.

" Would that the strength of my body were but equal
to the energy of my mind, methinks I would work won-
ders ; but alas ! it is not, and I must be content to waste
my time in large masses, lest my sublunary existence
should be the sacrifice of application. This is doleful ;
but many are in far worse plight than I am, both men-
tally and bodily, therefore I have good reason to be
thankful.

"As I have not strength for incessant exertion of any sort, I must let the plodders fag through the laborious processes of art and science, and do as well as I can by fits and starts with the means and opportunities God has given me.

"The occasion of the approaching change of pursuit seems to be the receipt to-day of No. 28 of the *Quarterly Review*, wherein there is a most flattering and encouraging critique upon my *Opera prima*. This doubtless is the immediate cause, though the remote one be my usual fickleness of disposition, which never allows me to stick long to any one pursuit. Some condemn this; others think it good. My own opinion is, that nature, when she strongly leans in any direction, is our best guide.

"Some men are pre-disposed for intense and long continued application to one object. Let them fag on. It is their bounden duty so to do. Others cannot apply themselves at all. This is a woeful extreme. They must continue blockheads.

"The class to which I belong is that which delights to follow an object *con furio* for a time, then to rest the faculties by a change to a different pursuit, calling other powers into exercise, and then to return to the former with increased zest and delight.

"So with me, Music is my leading or principal study; and this contains an amusing variety in itself; in practice, the mode of performance on various instruments, and the act of composition; in theory, the nature and variety and laws of Sound.

"But even this is not for me a sufficient range. Other objects occasionally present themselves, and I follow them with avidity, only to return to the master theme.

"After reading the news at the Philosophical Institution, I applied myself to the perusal of the article on *Acoustics*, in the Encyclopædia Britannica. It did not

please me, seeing it produces no other proof of the nature
of sound than the old experiment of a bell yielding none
in an exhausted receiver, which, it says, demonstrates that
it is a pulsation.

"I see that some vague notion of the connection of
sound with Electricity has been started, but not carried
out to constitute anything like a plausible hypothesis.

"I heard my son Handel read a little. He improves.
(æt. 4.)"

"January 23, 1826.

"What is the reason why *good taste* is to be so rarely
found in connection with *what is called* evangelical religion? Evangelical, surely *it is not*. It were blasphemy
to affirm that God would disapprove of Music, Poetry,
Painting or Sculpture, when pursued with a view to His
praise and glory. It were blasphemy to affirm that such
a Being could be properly worshipped through the medium of the nonsense found in many of the hymns. But
hold! perhaps, I judge rashly. If a man offer to his
Maker that which he esteems to be the best of its kind,
it will be accepted.

"Unanimity, perhaps, never will be attained, more
especially in matters of taste. But seriously, I contemplate the propriety of my renunciation of the office of
organist. It continually involves me in squabbles with
some party or other. Where so many are concerned, *all*
can never be satisfied, and the devil gets the vantage
ground, to raise disturbance; for those who are contented
with existing arrangements say nothing, and thus the
voices of a few, frequently repeated, pass for the voices
of the majority." ·

" January 30, 1826.

"In Park St. I was apprehended by two of the Committee of the Philosophical Institution who insisted upon

the expediency and propriety of my giving a lecture or course of lectures upon Music there.

"In the evening, I began a second time arranging my ideas for a series of lectures on Sound and Music.

"I find much difficulty in making them fall into any sort of order, the subjects branch out into so many different ways.

"Thus Music may be considered either as Melody or Harmony, or both united; either as plain or florid, as secular or sacred, as public or chamber, as national or universal, as vocal or instrumental, as natural or artificial; neither is it possible to reduce these to a regular *connected* order.

"For exercise I have recently thought of adopting a new idea, which is, to procure a good log of oak, and set to work at intervals to carve out of it *a chair*.

"Such an undertaking would serve to amuse me perhaps for years, and when complete might be handed down to my posterity as the work of their ancestor 'the Doctor!'

"When I reflect on the numerous projects, which my poor imagination has given rise to and my utter inadequacy to fulfil or execute them, I have a distinct and useful feeling of the vanity of earthly hopes and expectations.

"Nevertheless I will go on whilst my strength shall last, and though I live not to accomplish my projects, my hints may be of use to others, when I shall be no more seen."

"May 6, 1826.

"In reading Locke yesterday upon identity and diversity, a sudden thought came into my head of writing a work upon my idea of the possible occupation of separate spirits.

"I wish to infuse into the minds of the populace a more *merry* notion of Celestial happiness than the parsons allow them to entertain.

"I also thought of making the work a vehicle for some of my more extravagant thoughts upon Music; *e. g.* the infinite divisibility of musical intervals, and the boundless extent of the scale, the unlimited number of primes, and the celestial possibility of millions of real parts. Much of my work was to have been filled with conversations upon these subjects, between such men as Tubal-Cain and Handel.

" Then I had the wild thought of introducing the doctrine of Transmigration of souls, in such a manner as not to contradict any doctrine of Revelation, and to make adventures of this sort the source of much amusing dialogue above. So much for a passing thought.

"I read a goodly portion of Locke to-day, and continued at intervals to complete the accompaniments of my Duett, 'The God of Heaven shall set up a Kingdom.' The composition is not despicable, but it falls far short of my expectation."

" I begin, I perceive, to entertain a somewhat different notion of the cause of my last week's uneasiness to that which has for so many days made me miserable.

"I see in it now the chastising hand of a merciful Father. I was beginning to be puffed up. Church Music had been my study; perhaps I was resting on it. I had operated some small degree of improvement, and was almost in the daily receipt of adulatory congratulations on my success. I did not give God the glory as was His due. Let me never henceforth engage in any Divine Service without lifting up my heart to God for His gracious blessing on my humble efforts. I will work yet more in dependance upon Him, Whose I am, and Whom I desire to serve. I will continually implore His guidance, as well for the government of myself as for the management of my unruly fingers.

" I will yet more than ever despise that bubble reputation ; and seek only to gain the approbation of a conscience void of offence. Come what may I shall be armed. Anonymous scribblers may wear their pens out, and exhaust their inkstands ; I will by Divine help keep on the even tenor of my way.

" Yet a little while, and all will be over. All these discords of suspension will be resolved. There will be no squabbling about loudness or softness, intricacy or simplicity, variety or uniformity.

" All will be order. All will be peace."

One great individuality of my Father's mind, equally rare and valuable, is distinctly brought out in this thought of " Celestial Dialogues."

I refer to the union of technical knowledge—the machinery of parts as it were—with an almost boundless imagination. In most minds these are separare gifts. A *merely religious* mind would here have freely described what it believed would be a natural gratification of its highest faculties ; the soul would be filled with adoration, and occupied in music, embodying probably no higher idea of the latter than most people are able to form of it in *this* world.

But we see how the Scientific Musician comes in, with his expanded, God-given intellect, bringing a treasure of thought to those able to follow him. It

is almost impossible for us to realize what he means
—bound as we are by accepted and contracted notions of music (as well as of everything else !)—by
" the infinite divisibility of the usual intervals, the
boundless extent of the scale, the unlimited number
of primes, the celestial possibilities of millions of
real parts."

To *think* of all this seems impossible to *us ;* and
what a glimpse it gives us of the scientific and religious workings of his own mind ! How unique,
too, his choice of Tubal-Cain and Handel as holding a conversation ! It seems as though he were
still uniting in imagination two great representa-
tives, thrown apart by ages : one, the great worker
in metals, and the other the musician who has given
us in music the sublimest religious thought the
world has ever received.

His use of the word "merry," too, in connection
with the future occupation, is significant. Perhaps
he was driven to it by the narrow and contracted
theological teaching of his day, at which he frequently revolted.

Intellectual life and sublime thought were to him
inconsistent with lugubrious, dismal, pietistic religion.

From the Diary.

" October 1, 1829.

" I proceeded with my brother Archelaus to Redcliff
Church, where we witnessed the really astounding per-

formance of Samuel Wesley upon the noble organ there-in. It was the most wonderful I ever heard, more even than I had before been capable of conceiving ; the flow of melody, the stream of harmony, was so complete, so unbroken, so easy, and yet so highly wrought and so superbly scientific, that I was altogether knocked off my stilts. Before such a man and organist I am less than nothing and vanity. A Duett was performed by him and his son, Samuel Sebastian Wesley. The Concluding Fugue was sublime. A few Choruses and Songs were interspersed but I wished them away. Samuel, Edward, and George D. Fripp, besides a host of professional Organists were present, and were doubtless carried into the third Heaven. I exchanged a few words with the old man and his son on the performance being over. I walked home afterwards, but my head was full of naught but Samuel Wesley and his seraphic genius. I wrote a para-graph for the *Mirror*, laudatory of Mr. S. W. No words can sound his praises too highly. He is the Prince of Musicians and Emperor of Organists."

" October 4th.

" I performed two or three movements out of Sebastian Bach on my Piano, but was completely out of humour with my musicality. Why, however, should I repine ? Is it not as much a man's duty to be content with such in-tellectual powers as God may be pleased to impart to him, as it is to be satisfied with his rank and station in life ? God has made one man a Wesley, another a Hodges ; I pray for a grateful heart and humble spirit. Who knows whether Wesley's visit to Bristol be not ordered by divine goodness to detach me from the world, and to make me see that ' all is vanity and vexation of spirit ? '

" I thought myself something in *music* at least, but even that is taken from me.

" Yet I will endeavour to ' play before the Lord, and if
I have not the skill of an Arch-Angel, He will graciously
accept my more humble offering, and I will wait His good
pleasure to be enabled to praise Him in loftier strains
above.

" I got through my duties somehow (I will not say I
played the organ) at St. Nicholas' in the morning and at
St. James' in the afternoon and evening."

" October 5th.

" At one o'clock I hastened to Redcliff Church to witness Sam. Wesley's astonishing powers once more.   I was
of course delighted, but was not completely carried away
as I was on the former occasion.   The sinning sinners, or
singing singers came around me and accused me of being
the author of a paragraph in the papers, which spoke
slightingly of them.   I did not satisfy them."

They would have been less satisfied had they
been aware that the solemn young man who spoke
to them so courteously had in an " aside " called
them a motley group of bawlers and a sorry set of
scrubs.   The bills said an " effective choir."

" October 7th.

" I spent a very rattletrappish sort of morning, and
between twelve and one set forth in Wilkin's fly to
witness Mr. Wesley's third and last performance on the
organ.

" In this instance I did not experience so much gratification as upon either of the former occasions ; but cannot
be sure whether this arose from a sense of satiety in myself or a perception of a falling off (comparatively with
the preceding exhibitions) in him.

" In an article published in the Bristol *Mirror*, Oct. 4, I expressed the high sense which I, at the first performance, entertained of Mr. Wesley's superlative merits. Although somewhat bombastic and stiltified, it was the genuine production of the impressions made upon my mind and fancy."

I quote from the article :

" Mr. Wesley's performance upon the organ at Redcliff Church was of such a nature as to baffle all powers of description.   His splendid extemporaneous effusions left his hearers perfectly astounded.   Such concatenations of splendid harmonies passed through the noble vaultings of that venerable pile, as can alone be produced by the highest efforts of genius, inspired by Divine enthusiasm, in man or angel.   The effect was literally superhuman. Seldom indeed does it fall to mortal lot to witness such a sublime exhibition of seraphic skill.   In a duett by Mr. Wesley and his son the climax of the concluding Fugue was grand beyond conception ; the imagination of the hearers was necessarily over-whelmed with ideas of immensity and infinity, and the stupendous powers of the magnificent instrument upon which the father and son were exerting, but evidently not exhausting, their talents were absorbed and totally forgotten in the melodious torrent, which seemed as it were to sweep ' all Heaven's harmonies before it.'   On such an occasion praise and ' puff ' are alike futile and superfluous."

His Diary proceeds :

" Now that I have heard the great man two or three times, I can begin to analyse, not only my own sensations, but the means by which he contrives to excite them and it may be well to record an observation or two on the subject.

" *Wonder* never can be permanent.

" I was at first taken by surprise by Wesley's exceedingly full harmonies, many of which seemed to be incomprehensible ; by the march of his modulations, which seemed almost incapable of detection ; by the incessant flow of apparently new melodies, which seemed to emanate from an exhaustless source ; and by the delicate rapidity and precision of his complex execution, which seemed to defy human rivalry.

" But these points successively either vanished altogether, or were lowered somewhat nearer to the ordinary range of mortal ability, on every successive hearing ; towards the end, indeed, in almost every succeeding piece performed. The full harmonies all resolved themselves into the classes into which I am distributing them in my ' Tentamen,' [1] viz. either *Diatonic* or *Chromatic Mixtures*, and had been rendered at first inappreciable by me, because I was not sufficiently accustomed to the precise pitch of that particular organ, to determine what were the notes actually sounding. Thus my imagination wandered through a host of keys without attaching a definite notational idea to any one of them.

" Now, much of this was gone on the second performance taking place, and all was removed long before the third was over, still his harmonies were fine and masterly.

" Again, from a similar cause, his bold modulations were at first astounding, because mysterious ; but they anon became familiar, though used with unwonted skill. Still it might not have been the skill of a genius of the third Heaven.

" The flow of melody is also a point in which Wesley did not maintain his first impressions ; for many of the

[1] An exhaustive work on Thorough Bass.

passages occurred over and over again. Yet was there enough of novelty on each occasion to entitle him to the praise of lofty imagination. And lastly his execution, which perhaps was the best (or at least second best) point of his performance, seemed on further investigation to be perfectly attainable by a little regular practice, combined with the attainment of a sound knowledge of Harmony. Thus, bit by bit, it would appear as though all his merit was to be frittered down to the ordinary level of humanity. Not so, however, or more than one Samuel Wesley would be discoverable in the world. He must be ranked as a man of superlative talent and first-rate genius.

"But notwithstanding all this, I shall come to a little closer criticism yet. His grand forte is confessedly *extempore fugue*. The subjects are generally bold and striking, the opening clear and well compacted together *secundum artem*, the organ-points towards the end skilfully introduced, and worked up with the most scientific harmonies, and the concluding cadences characteristic and effective.

"But lo! the subjects themselves seemed to be but illegitimate offsprings of Sebastian Bach, (Sam. Wesley's idol,) and the opening of each fugue has doubtless been well studied."

"Samuel Wesley, the Prince of Organists," was the toast given by my Father at a dinner-party, October 12 1829, in Bristol, on the occasion of his meeting Dr. Wesley, whom he does not hesitate to call, "The first organist in the world." Around were seated many of the choicest spirits of Bristol, and when my Father rose and proposed the toast, it was received and drunk with enthusiasm.   He writes: "Mr. Wesley was visibly effected. It gladdened the heart of the old man," who was, my Father knew, at that time in trouble.

"Cloisters, October 28, 1829.

"Between eight and nine Wesley came to breakfast and both before and after that meal, I amused him by showing him some of my Musical Conundrums.   He flattered and encouraged me.   He begged me to go on with my Anthem for the King; and added that it was, as far as done, really good; and added, morever that Attwood never could have written such a chorus as that beginning, 'Thou O King, art a King of Kings.'   He commended my style for strength."

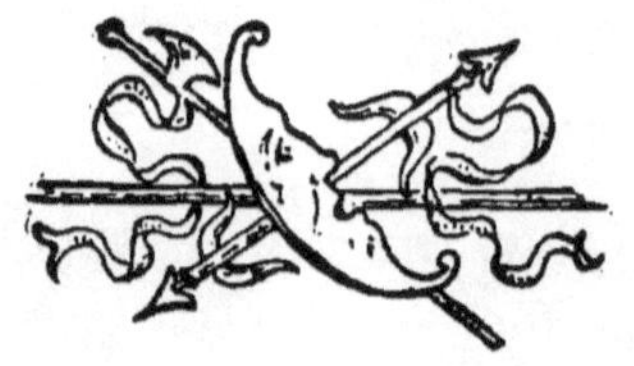

CHAPTER V.

THE year 1834 was a time of domestic sorrow. The long-continued illness of my Mother incapacitated my Father for any heavy or continuous mental work, and his energies went out in diligent, unselfish actions, visiting and caring for his aged and sick relatives, and bringing comfort to many others in their sickness and sorrow,—and in quiet reading and study at home.

My dear Mother died on the Feast of St. Michael and All Angels, 1835, at the age of thirty-five, believing surely that she would meet us again, and knowing Him faithful in Whom she trusted.

I quote again from the diary :

"*St. James' Church, Dec. 25, 1834.*

"During the morning service I felt at a loss for an appropriate L. M. Tune, and composed one, principally whilst the Nicene Creed was being read (the idea did not occur to me to write one at all until the minister began the Gospel for the day) of which I had time only to set down hastily the Bass.

"I made for Handel a rough copy in pencil whilst the

Clerk was giving out the first verse, which I completed as
he gave out the second, and the little fellow sang it at
sight bravely. Such an occurrence as this does not happen
every day, and therefore, although a trifle, it deserves to
be recorded."

" Sunday, December 6, 1835.

" Before I left home after dinner I made the children
sing a few notes for Thomas Cook to hear them. On this
occasion Miriam exhibited a truly astonishing compass of
voice, viz., four Octaves! from F, the bass clef note, to F
in altissimo. Sebastian's was very nearly the same, but
he could not reach either of the extremes so well as his
sister.

" Both Faustina's and Jubal's voices are of shorter
compass."

" Perhaps it is a good thought that I cannot better
employ a portion of the little property which has recently
fallen to me than by endeavouring to increase my professional reputation, which if it may not ultimately benefit
me, may have a reflective and beneficial effect upon the
prospects of my children.

" I will think about it, and probably consult my friend
Havergal.

" I have several ponderous Anthems which I should
like to bring out ; but will people condescend to purchase
them? There 's the rub."

*A reflective effect upon the prospects of my chil-
dren !* True in his grand unselfishness, his humility,
and his prophetic spirit !

Regarding myself, where in the world could a
duty have been more plainly indicated than mine ?
And in the discharge of it, little as I have been

able to do, I have had a happiness in sending one gleam—one "reflected" gleam of my own prosperity and success back to their generous and undoubted source.

To return to the Diary :

" In the evening I brought up this account and turned over a few pages of music. Thus passed a comparatively unprofitable close of a (shall I say ?) misspent day. No. No day is altogether misspent, in which a frail mortal has been made more sensible than before of his frailty.

" And yet, with this increased consciousness of frailty, I found myself frail still—"

One of my Father's strongest characteristics was his love and reverence for his Father.

In the sketch of his own life (in his Grandfather's Bible), after noting his own baptism, he has written :

" The register thereof will be found in the Bristol Tabernacle (for his Father was a Dissenter, albeit a good man nevertheless)."

All who remember my Father would here trace his vein of natural humour.

In his Journals he marks the " Translation " of his saintly departed by a crown and initials.

" Nov. 6, 1834.

" The Anniversary of my good Father's translation. May I be enabled to follow him as far as he followed Christ, and by God's good grace, with him to inherit the promises.

"Three and twenty years of labour and sorrow have elapsed since his decease, but they have been also three and twenty years of mercy and loving-kindness.

"I have seen a little during that period, and endeavoured to *observe* what I saw ; but behold! 'All was vanity and vexation of spirit !'

"The course of the world is in itself, and abstracted from all proofs else derived, a sufficient indication that this state of being is not the ultimate condition of an immortal being. I express myself badly. Here good and evil are mixed without any apparent reference to moral attributes in the man, as they would assuredly be in a state of probation.

"Hence this state is not final."

"Aug. 7, 1835.

"Faustina's birthday.

"The Lord preserve her and keep her alive that she may be blessed upon earth."

Was it not answered to the full ?—F. H. H.

"Jan. 31, 1836.

"Thou who wast tempted *in all points* (Oh ! the unspeakable comfort of such a passage !) like as we are, 'yet *without sin.*' Amen, and Amen.

"No. Temptation is *not* sin. I thank God for that.

"'Blessed is the man that endureth temptation, for when he is tried he shall receive the crown of life which the Lord hath promised to them that love Him.'"

My Father as a general rule summarised his works and progress at the end of every month, often passing upon himself the most severe and searching criticism and judgment.

The life that *we* saw needed not this indeed, these words in the form of a prayer, occurring amongst his serious thoughts at the age of twenty-seven :

" Enable me so to act that I bring no descredit upon myself or the Profession of Godliness."

Diary.

"*Feb. 27, 1836.*

" Mr. Bunt wished me to undertake a Secretaryship to one of the Sections of the British Association (to meet in Bristol next summer,) but I declined it."

" *Cloisters, Aug. 1, 1836.*

" T. G. Bunt came in after dinner, and told me that my name had been proposed as a member of the British Association, I being a scientific individual, entitled to admission without further payment than the customary small annual subscription ; and that it had been unanimously agreed to ; some gentlemen having volunteered to speak very favourably of my character and attainments !

" So far, so good ; but it was all done without my knowledge or sanction."

The following sweet significant picture is a characteristic sketch of my Father among church bells ; one of the very rare glimpses we get of him as a schoolboy :—on a Sunday, too !

" *Bristol, April 23, 1836.*"

After describing a busy morning in the city he says :

"I walked off towards Kingsdown. On my way I fell in with Mr. T. G. Bunt, and prevailed on him to accompany to St. Matthew's Church (newly erected). There we ascended the steeple, in order to inspect the operations going on in hanging the peal of eight bells presented by old Mr. Bangley. We spent a considerable time there, and the men were so civil as to lift the tenor bell from the planks on which it rested, in order that we might hear its tone, which strongly reminded me of that of Chelwood Church, when I was a school-boy and used to amuse myself as I sat in the chancel on a cold stone seat by forming harmonies to it with my voice. One of the men said the note was E. Mr. Bunt thought F. The weight is nearly 21 cwt. and that of the whole peal 78 cwt."

On a cold stone seat in the chancel of the old village church, and his mind at work on harmonies as he listened to the bell from the tower !

To continue from the Diary :

"Cloisters, May 9, 1836.

"Another exhilarating morning. I could not find it in my heart to *waste* such a day by sticking to my desk, so I put on my hat (no great coat however) and marched out. After making an appointment with John Smith for to-morrow, I directed my course to Clifton, through that delightful parish to the verge of Durdham Down, and so by the Turnpike road to the side of the River, the tide just flowing. I truly enjoyed the ramble and felt grateful adoration towards the Giver of all good.

"At and about the Hotwells I tarried for a considerable time (two hours I suppose), witnessing many steam boat motions, and the departure of a large American Brig (the *Tuscany*) full of emigrants, towed down against

CLIFTON.

wind and tide by the two new steam Tugs the *Lioness* and the *Fury*. From the Wells I departed by the bank of the new course of the Avon and so across Prince's Bridge into the city."

My Father's graphic description of one walk is an indication of his enjoyment of the hundreds of rambles he took to Rownham and St. Vincent's Rocks. Here was not only a grand manifestation of the forces of Nature in the upheaval and rending of the Rocks—a truly imposing sight—but away and beyond towards the Avonmouth, where at the Channel it joins the Severn, there is a richness and varied beauty of green and woodland, trending down to the water level, and an expanse of view which no other city affords. At this time the second seaport in the kingdom, the shores of its water-way were a delightful resort. It was a beautiful, as well as a suggestive sight at the flow of the tide, to watch the ships and steamers passing up and down the river, whose winding course doubled its distance from Cumberland Basin to the Channel.

Added to this, my Father had opportunity for the indulgence of his favourite study of Mechanics in various ways; for carrying on his observations, and thinking out his own thoughts, about steam engines, and propellers, and paddle wheels, and

mud removers, and dock gates, and all other mechanical contrivances in which his heart delighted.

"January 18, 1837.

" I put in at Fletcher's office and at length obtained
an interview with that gentleman. I mentioned the circumstance that I had a railway improvement idea to dis-
pose of, and my wish to bring it before the Coal Pit
Heath R. R. Comp. (of which F. is secretary), referring
to Mr. Brunel for a character of the invention, but without describing it. It was agreed that I should write a
letter to Mr. F. which he promised to lay before the
Committee on Friday.

" At four I dined at a party at W. H. Baily's. Did
not get home till nearly midnight. Took up Buckland's
Treatise and finished it."

"April 14, 1837.

" I learned a piece of intelligence which is far from
giving me pleasure, viz. that a Patent has been taken out
by some man for an invention to do away with the necessity of employing stationary or assistant power in ascending inclined planes on Railroads. Most probably it is
identical with my invention herein recorded (though I
believe not described) and which I communicated several
months ago to Mr. Brunel. My inventions have almost
invariably been claimed by other people."

" Cogitanda.

"Dec. 31, 1836.

"In taking a review of the past year, I cannot but feel
most sensibly that life is a dream, and that all 'things
temporal' are but shadows at the best, conducing only
to 'vanity and vexation of spirit.' Not indeed that my
lot is or has been particularly hard, although I may some-

times be foolish enough to fancy so ; but in the course of
my forty years' experience, the sentiment just declared
has continually gained ground upon me until it has attained the authority of settled conviction. Still I can
enjoy the good things of this life as well as most men,
and I hope that I can enjoy them with gratitude to the
'Giver of all good.' Certainly my life hitherto has been
a life of continued trial ; but my hope is *above*. This is
not in any sense my 'continuing city.' All the troubles
which I have experienced have, as I confidently trust,
been administered or permitted in mercy and in love, by
Him who cannot err. Notwithstanding this comfortable
dependence, whilst I am *here* I must feel with humanity,
and in no year of my earthly sojourn have I felt more
acutely than in that now just on the point of terminating,
that all things here are precarious and transitory, illusory
in prospect and deceitful in possession. Perhaps of all
the shades and descriptions of experience in life, that is
the most favourable to the idea of earthly good, in which
there is the greatest quantity of ungratified hope. If so,
my lot has fallen amongst the most happy !"

" November 6, 1851.

"Forty years ago my Father, then ten years younger
than I am now, was translated into the world of spirits.
And it is now a few days more than thirty-eight years
since my Mother was likewise taken away.

"Good Lord ! so teach me to number my days that I
may apply my heart unto wisdom."

There was a simple dignity about my Father's
hour of Evening Prayer. At ten o'clock the little
family assembled. His " Grandfather's Bible " was
brought in from the study on a a cushion by one of

his sons and placed before him ; the cushion was for him to kneel on. The rays from the lamp falling on his thoughtful and reverent countenance, his exquisite reading, and the light thrown on the chosen chapter by his intelligent study of the Sacred Text, and the emphasis that study indicated, made my Father's reading of the Bible a memory to be treasured all one's life.

I have said that my Father chanted (or as he liked to say and write, *Chaunted*) the "Nunc Dimittis" the last thing before he retired at night.

This was one of the most exquisitely plaintive prayers one could listen to.

In December, 1835, my Father made a short visit to London. The rapidity of his movements on these occasions, the number of visits he made and the amount of ground he got over, are truly astonishing.

I will select a few of his most interesting entries ; Cooper and Attwood were the Organists at St. Paul's Cathedral and the Chapel Royal (St. James's) respectively.

"*Dec.* 7.

"Snow has been fast falling hitherto all the morning. I went into the city and lounged semi-studiously at the Commercial Rooms.

"I penetrated as far as the Temple Church in the evening and attended Divine Service. The organ was managed lamely and tamely and lifelessly enough. Cogan preached a good sermon from the text 'Who is this?' I sat in one of the free seats at the bottom of the church. As I entered the church they were reading the Psalms. The first words which caught my ear were, 'Dwell in the land and verily thou shalt be fed,' (*Ps. xxxvii*) the same with which a poor old deranged woman addressed me as I entered the Cathedral; a phrase also which both the late Mrs. Weare and my late aunt Elizabeth Hodges frequently enforced on my attention when I talked of the necessity of my removing from my native city. On the present occasion the words fastened themselves strongly upon my mind, and many other passages of the same Psalm seemed to be expressly intended for my comfort and encouragement. It was this which induced me to take a seat and hear the whole Service, for I had wandered into the Porch idly, merely to hear a bar or two of the organ playing.

"May the good Lord realize in my experience this gracious promise for His Mercy's sake. Amen."

"Friday, December 11th.

"Lunched with Cooper at his house. Afterwards went to St. Paul's. Service chaunted. Spent the evening at Baily's. Cooper there also, and looked over some of my Anthems.

"12th. Call on Flight. Visit to a soup-shop, long ditto to the 'Gallery of Practical Science.' Dined at Baily's. Collard there in the evening.

"13th. Sunday. At. St. Paul's at the morning and afternoon service. 'Played out' at the latter, as also at St. Sepulchre's in the morning, and the Percy Chapel in the evening. Dined with Cooper, made a miserable meal. The fault not *his*. Attwood very hearty and cordial, and in love with the idea of my *Organ Swell*.

" 14th.   Nothing to be done with Paine and Hopkins about the publication of my ' Church Reform ' Anthem. Went to Mill-Wall, Poplar, to look for Mr. Seaward to confer about my steam-boat project.   Conversation with Capt. McArthur on a stage coach on my way back.   At St. Paul's at three o'clock.   Played the ' Nunc Dimittis.' Cooper and Baily dined with me at the Percy at five. Cooper to tea also.   Concert by the Society of British Musicians at the Hanover Square Rooms.   Cooper supt with me afterwards.

" 15th . . .   Paine and Hopkins refuse to publish for me unless entirely at my own risque.   At St. Paul's in the afternoon.   My A♭ chaunt done.   Altered and spoilt. Flight called in the evening.   I showed him the Steamer Model and took him to Baily's, where we spent a merry evening with Cooper, etc., etc.

" 16th.   Wednesday.   Morning spent with Flight, principally at the Adelaide Gallery of Practical Science. Called on C. C. Clarke.   Dined at Baily's.   Took a share (10 guis.) in his lottery for a superb statue called ' The Sleeping Nymph.'

" 17th.   Packed up and left London by nine.

" At Windsor by eleven.   Chat with French, etc. Chapel visited.   Off to Maidenhead.   Dined with Mr. and Miss Atkinson.

" Slept at the Bear.   Off at ten for Bath.   Arrived there at 7 P.M.   Spent the evening at Mrs. Gibbs' cheerfully.   Slept at the Greyhound.   Left Bath as soon as I had swallowed my breakfast and reached home before noon.

" 19th.   Since my arrival at home I have unpacked my travelling baggage and delivered to my children certain little toys which I purchased for them in London."

(On hearing of the death of Dr. Clark-Whitfeld, Professor of Music, Cambridge.)

" Feb. 27 1836.

" The vacant Professorship of Cambridge has excited (but very gradually) no little ambitious feeling in my heart. Yet what vanities are all worldly distinctions! Shall I however be content to occupy but a low position? As a servant of the Most High, I feel that I may lawfully aspire to such a position in society as in His good providence may be within my reach, trusting that He will grant me the grace to use what honour may accrue to me for the promotion of His glory and the good of my fellow creatures.

" If it be not His will that I should attain the post now unoccupied, vain will be my attempt. I hope that I have by *this* time learnt a little of true and unfeigned *resignation*. This methinks a man may have, under defeat, and yet not be blind to the circumstance (if so it were) that as far as *man* was concerned he had been unjustly dealt with."

" Oct. 28, 1837.

" The affection of my eyes still continuing, I have meditated upon the posibility of my becoming *blind*, and endeavoured to commit a fugue (a short one in D minor by Sebastian Bach) to *memory*. This is with me a matter of intense difficulty. I have never yet been able to play Memoriter more than a few Chaunts, Psalm-tunes and simple melodies."

As far as I know my Father suffered only from over-straining his eyes.

Regarding what he says of himself, the question arises how could so creative a mind as his, one so

full of the power not only of fugue extemporisation
—and that thoroughly in all the parts—but of the
ability to write elaborate fugues of three subjects—
how could such a mind feel disposed to memorize
similar compositions even by a *greater* mind ? Are
there not existing antagonistic mental powers ? It
would be interesting to follow up this enquiry ;
whether the greatest fugue *writers* were also the
greatest fugue *players*, or were not, simply because
they might not have had the time to give to the
necessary study which committal requires.

The mental power of musicians may be as varied
as their faces—no two alike.

We all know that the best of memories may at the
merest trifle, the stir even of an insect's wing, prove
treacherous and untrustworthy ; and the very fact
of his *reverence* for his two great masters made him,
if possible, more artistically true to them. It was
remarkable how distinct he kept the great mind he
was rendering from his own powers as composer.
In the one case he was, as it were, in the traces of
truth and honour to *another ;* he was the " voice
of one " speaking through *his* mind and fingers
with renewed life ; but when he spoke of *himself*
at his organ, in prelude and fugue, in mysterious
grandeur or spiritual meditation, or in the exaltation of the " Hallelujah," when his thoughts were

inspired by the service, when people stood transfixed in the aisles, as the gorgeously coloured light from the windows fell through the church : then it was that his Pegasus was free ; and, bounding above our limited imaginary views, he struck the mountain-tops in the lightness of his footfall, seeming to pass the clouds themselves, and to take his way to the very Source of life and genius, of sacred song and aspiration.

What need had he to memorize? he, whose perennial fount of fresh improvization, or meditation, or jubilization was so grand and exhaustible?

Never shall I forget the sound of his exquisite fugue-playing as I treasure it on one particular occasion. It was after the *Great Western* had brought my sweet sister Miriam, and myself, to New York in the summer of 1841.

We were all living, ourselves and our newly-found Father, near St. John's Park, in the house of Mr. Charles Horn, grandson of a former organist of the Chapel Royal, Windsor, and son of Mr. Charles E. Horn, the fascinating singer of Beethoven's " Adelaide " and composer of " Cherry Ripe " and lots of taking unforgetables in popular music ; and the two actresses, daughters of Wallack, (then, I believe, a leading man on the stage) were there also.

CHAPTER VI.

IN March, 1835, a vacancy having occurred in
the post of Organist at St. George's Chapel,
Windsor, my Father became a candidate for the
position. From a warm friend of both the com-
batants I received the following account of the
competition that took place for the appointment,
the facts being given to him by one who was
present on the occasion.

"It appears that there were no less than thirty-two
applicants of every degree and kind, J. B. Knight, the
ballad writer, being one of them. The number, after a
partial trial of nearly all, was reduced to twelve, then to
six, then to four, and finally the Dean and Chapter
decided upon two candidates, Dr. Edward Hodges and
George J. Elvey, each of whom was required to accompany the choir at one of the services, with the privilege
of selecting both Service and Anthem used on the occasion. Mr. Salmon told me that your Father played
'Gibbons in F,' and the Anthem by Boyce; and his
accompaniments were greatly admired by the choir and
congregation. The following day young Elvey's turn
came. He was only nineteen, and had many friends and

admirers; and his brother, Dr. Stephen Elvey, was at that time Organist of New College, Oxford. When the Dean and Chapter met for their decision, objection was made to Elvey's youth, but it was over-ruled by the majority, on the ground that he would be easier to manage than Dr. Hodges. A majority of the Chapter thought the latter candidate would be more desirable ; and here again the Dean interposed by saying he did not fancy the broad-brimmed hat and white necktie, and boots with pointed toes, suggesting to him an individuality that might prove difficult to control—and all this happened nearly fifty years ago. Every one of the chief actors has passed off this stage of life, and Elvey alone remains! When he goes we shall have seen and heard the last of the true type of thoroughbred Cathedral Organists and Musicians.

" Mr. Salmon, in speaking of your Father's accompaniments with unstinted praise, said to me : ' Dr. Hodges had a very difficult task before him in having to play on an F manual Organ with an F pedal keyboard when for many years he had been accustomed to a C manual and pedal.' You of course know that the Organ in St. James's Church, Bristol was the first CC manual and CCC pedal keyboard made in England ; and if I remember rightly, it had a 16-foot stopped pipe, speaking the 32-feet tone. Among my books was a volume issued as long ago as 1843, containing exclusively your Father's compositions, and among them his ' Morning and Evening Service in C,' and the Anthem especially written for the opening of St. James's Organ. Sir George Elvey told me that he did not dare to play in public upon a C manual and pedal, he could take no *big chords* with his left hand (G and A, for instance) and he was constantly putting down the CCC pedal key, thinking it was the FFF. While speaking about Organs I may tell you that the late Dr. S. S. Wesley said to me that a G manual with G sharp was the proper compass for all Organs ; but in *all cases*, there should be a C pedal keyboard. I think he was right."

It was in the glorious Chapel of St. George, so truly called " Royal," rich in its storied heraldry of kings and emperors, where the very air, that hardly sways the banners that hang there, is filled with the religious loyalty of England, where the Royal Standard floats before the rich organ case, where the iridescent gleams of light from painted window tint and touch cornice, capital, or column, or fall athwart some exquisite monument or tomb, that the contest for the office of organist took place. My Father himself tells the story of it in his diary in the cloistered seclusion of his own home :

" May 22, 1835.

" On Monday evening (past 10 o'clock), March 2, 1835, on my return from a chess party I received a letter from Mrs. Pigott, announcing the death of my friend *Skeats*, the Organist of St. George's Chapel, Windsor, couched in such terms as left no doubt that it was the dying wish of the deceased officer that I might succeed him. With the customary misfortune attending anything connected with my interests, strange to say this letter (which in due course of the post ought to have been delivered at my house by 10 A.M.) had been ' missent to Westbury,' the consequence of which was that it was not delivered until evening, and *I lost the whole day*. Perhaps

ST. GEORGE'S CHAPEL, WINDSOR.

this delay may have occasioned some of the (so-called) ill-luck which followed, although doubtless all was ' ordered aright ' by the great Disposer of events.

" I prepared for my journey the next morning, moved off in the evening by the Mail Coach, reached Windsor early on Wednesday (the first day of Lent,) made a very favorable impression the next day by a little preliminary performance upon the organ, left my Testimonials, from 1 to 51 inclusive, for the inspection of the Chapter, and returned home to await a summons to appear there again for a more formal exhibition of my talent as a player.

" In due course I received a letter from Mr. de St. Croix, Chapter Clerk, appointing Thursday, the ninth of April, for my performing exhibition.

" I accordingly went to Windsor again (reaching it on the 8th) and on the morning of the appointed day I performed the whole of the musical service. (Gibbons in F, and Boyce's noble Anthem, ' O where shall wisdom be found ? ') from score. Afterwards I played for an hour various pieces of music and extempory movements ; and when I had concluded, received the congratulations and commendations of two or three members of the Chapter, who spoke in such a vein as clearly conveyed the impression that they looked upon me as their future officer.

" However, all this was vain and illusory. I returned home full of flattering expectation that I was now at length just about to attain the object of my long formed wishes. The election was to take place on Monday, April 27, 1835, and did so ; but not myself but a young man named *George Elvey* was elected."

The following letters, bearing upon the subject of the election, are of interest.

From the Rev. Canon Bowles, A.M., of Brem-
hill to the Rev. R. Musgrave, of Windsor.

Canonry House, Salisbury, March 14, 1835.

"My Dear Sir,

"Dr. Hodges, of Bristol, one of the most scientific and
practical Musicians in England, as composer, as well as a
most skilfull organist, is anxious to obtain the post of
Organist at Windsor Castle Chapel. I say this from some
knowledge and the most fervent love of this Art, as the
powerful auxiliary to our affecting Cathedral services.

"His compositions in this line are sublime and affecting, and I am equally sure I can equally recommend him
as an exemplary and pious character and admirable
player.

"You will, I am sure, put forward as far as shall be in
your power among your Chapter-brethren this summary
of his merits,

"And believe me ever sincerely,

"W. M. Bowles."

From the Rev. R. Musgrave, Canon of Windsor, to the Rev. Canon Bowles of Salisbury.

"May 7, 1835.

"My Dear Sir,

"I trust you will not think me remiss in having suffered your letter to remain so long unanswered. But I
was unwilling to write to you till I could communicate
the result of the contest for the vacant situation of
Organist at Windsor.

"I need not say that I lost no time in forwarding your
high testimonial of Dr. Hodges' merits (who, as I am told,
performed Luther's Hymn in the most affecting and beautiful manner) to the Chapter.

" There were several other most highly talented Candidates—young men of excellent character, upon one of whom the election devolved, a Mr. Elvey from Oxford, whose merit I think will not be lessened by the circumstance of Dr. Hodges' having said that he thought him one of the most talented young performers he had ever heard. I need not assure you what pleasure it would have afforded me had the election terminated according to the wishes expressed by one whose sound judgment and beautiful taste in Cathedral music is so universally and justly appreciated.

" Always with great truth,

" R. MUSGRAVE."

Part of a letter from Mr. French, one of the gentlemen of the Choir of the Chapel Royal of St. George.

" Windsor, May 16, 1835.

" To Dr. Hodges.

" MY DEAR SIR,

" I am at a loss to conjecture how your professional talent can at all suffer from your not being appointed here.

" Your performance was highly approved by all, and your talent as an Organist and Composer stands too high in the musical world to lose one jot from the disappointment which you lay so much to heart,

" Many thanks for the pamphlets.

" I remain dear Sir,

" Yours truly,

" JOSIAH FRENCH."

The " Pamphlets " included one which Canon

Bowles styled my Father's " Admirable Defence of Church Music."

From W. de St. Croix, Chapter Clerk of Windsor Chapel Royal.

" Windsor, May, 1835.

" To Dr. Hodges.

" I sincerely sympathize with you under the disappointment you have experienced at the result of the election, but you well know that 'the race is not always to the swift.'

" Your performance of Luther's Hymn has made an impression in favour of your musical talents that will long be remembered by those who were so fortunate as to be present at your trial; and the favourable terms in which you expressed yourself respecting the merits of a rival Candidate, so far from operating to your disadvantage, was considered most honourable, generous, and disinterested conduct on your part, and met with the applause to which such handsome conduct was entitled.

" I remain Sir,

" Your faithful and obedient servant,

" W. DE ST. CROIX.

" Dr. EDWARD HODGES, Bristol."

From the Diary :

Saturday, June 18, 1835.

" Soon after I reached the house I chanced to take up " Felix Farley," and almost the first thing I observed was a notice of the decease of Mr. Paddon, Organist of Exeter Cathedral. This suddenly stirred me up to think of making another attempt to secure such a post as he has vacated, but I confess that I have very little notion of succeeding at Exeter, neither have I so strong an inclination to reside in that city, as I had to effect a settlement at Windsor.

"However, 'not as I will.' As a matter of duty I resolved to make some inquiries upon the subject, and accordingly I waited upon Mr. Martin (an Exeter man) in the evening, and obtained from him some particulars as to the names of some of the officers of the Cathedral. He read me a paragraph from the Exeter newspaper, wherein the Editor states his understanding that the office of organist is to be thrown open to free competition, and that Sir George Smart is to be appointed umpire or judge on the occasion. If so, there will be no hope for me. One of his own pupils will be sure to gain the appointment. However, I resolved to write to Exeter for official information as to the nature of the proceedings to be adopted, and accordingly, when I came home, I wrote a letter to Ralph Barnes, Esq., the Chapter-Clerk, asking a few questions and stating my desire to become a candidate provided the election is to be conducted upon the just ground of the general qualifications and character of the candidates, and not upon the mere agility of their fingers."

"*July 31st.*

"I received a letter from Exeter this morning. It was from Mr. Barnes, couched in the kindest possible terms, to inform me that the Chapter of Exeter had come to the decision to prefer two candidates before me, one of whom had been bred up in a Cathedral Choir, and the other had had the management of such a body. (I instantly fixed upon Dixon and young Wesley as the two parties referred to.) This communication had a strange effect upon my spirits. I felt horribly depressed, not that the choice had not fallen upon me, but that the reason now tactily assigned was the defect of my education as not being a *Cathedralite*.

"Well! well! my Master can yet provide for me, but it would seem as though it were not to be in *my own* way.

"I went into town and read the papers."

After an interval my Father continues :

"The Exeter Cathedral appointment is not to be conferred upon me, and for this reason, because I am not a Cathedral-bred man. If the objection be valid it shuts up my prospects *for life*. Aye more. It consigns me to an early grave. Not that I am now in danger of committing suicide, but that I am convinced that I am not calculated by constitution to contend with an uninterrupted course of vexatious circumstances. Character and qualifications seem to have been allowed to be proved to the fullest extent (saving only practical demonstration, and I begin to regret that this was not had recourse to), yet my pretensions were unceremoniously set aside, without a trial, because I did not have the happiness (shall I say misfortune?) to be trained under a Cathedral Organist, a man who for the greater part neglects his duty, and leaves the services to be conducted by any scrub who can get *through* with them. The thing galls me, and notwithstanding the marked politeness and kind attention of Mr. Barnes, the Chapter-Clerk of Exeter, a man who though unknown I begin to *love*, does not increase my affection for Deans and Chapters generally, who seem to be actuated by a very queer set of motives."

July 31st.

"It chanced that on entering my study this morning, I noticed a large black, and strange bird in the Bishop's Garden beneath my windows. On enquiry I found he

had been seen there several hours. In the course of the
morning I sent for the key of the garden, in order to ex-
amine the bird, to ascertain why it continued there, as it
appeared to be unable to fly, and not very expert in *hop-
ping* about.

"The key could not be obtained, but Mr. Crook hap-
pening to come in, he undertook to scale the garden wall
by the help of my ladder, and after a diligent search,
found the poor bird in a dark corner of the ruins of the
Bishop's Palace, and brought him in. We placed him in
a cage I had brought for a pair of doves several years ago.
The bird proved to be in very good condition, rather tame
than otherwise, but to have *lost one foot!* I thought it
was a Raven, but on reference to a book on Natural History we agreed to pronounce it a *crow*, as it had not the
dimensions assigned to the former. The fellow ate and
drank heartily and did not appear incommoded by its
imprisonment.

"Now this little occurrence suggested to my mind an
odd fancy, in the shape of an analogical prophecy. I had
two Cathedral organs in prospect, as the bird had doubtless originally two feet. But he has lost one of them. So
have I. His leg or ankle, however, betrays no wound, the
bird is none the worse for it. Why should I be for *my*
loss? The remaining leg and foot are sound and ser-
viceable. Perhaps my remaining leg may be trustworthy
yet! Who knows? Should Sam Wesley gain his point
at Exeter, how the bull will run at Hereford! But what
fancies do I run into! Does Providence intimate its will
by the intervention of crows or ravens? Truly it may:
for *God* sent the ravens to feed his prophet, and he may
have sent a crow to comfort me in my disappointment."

Aug. 14th.

"After I had discharged my customary morning en-
gagements, I wrote a letter to Mr. Barnes of Exeter,

thanking him for the very great kindness evinced in his correspondence, and at the same time venturing to contravene (as far as written words can) the principle laid down by the Chapter of Exeter, as operating to my exclusion from all competition for the situation of Cathedral Organist. This I did first by direct attack on the maxim, as being one which could only be proved or disproved by experiment, and next by adverting to some facts in my personal history not hitherto brought forward.

" It is barely possible that, if the Chapter have not come to a definite decision, this letter may reach their hands ; and that in that case it may produce some small effect on their minds. But the greater probability is, that the matter has been, ere this, definitely settled."

" *August 17, 1835.*

" In the Cloister I found a letter awaiting me from Exeter, wherein Mr. Barnes informs me that the Chapter have elected Mr. Wesley of Hereford."

After hearing of Wesley's election, my father sent his testimonials to Hereford.

CHAPTER VII.

LAST YEARS IN BRISTOL.

FROM the Bristol *Mirror :*

" February, 1836.

" The organ of St. Stephen's Church now building by Mr. John Smith the younger, under the superintendence of Dr. Hodges, is rapidly approaching completion, and, although not large, promises to be a superior instrument, embodying all the latest improvements."

The Anthem, *Ps. 136,* which I have denominated a prince among my Father's compositions, was performed at the opening of St. Stephen's organ, regarding which ceremony, as well as the composition of the Anthem, I give a few interesting particulars from the Diary.

" Jan. 25, 1836.

" I made a fair commencement of an anthem *(Ps. 136),* and, with intermission, continued the employment until 11 P.M.

" Jan. 27, 1836.

" In the evening I worked again at my new anthem and made a little progress, but laboured under too much real sadness to prosecute such an undertaking with likeli-

hood of success or rapidity.   I wish the composition to
be *cheerful*, yet my heart is in heaviness.   My way is altogether shut in.   I cannot get forth."

On the subject of organs everywhere, in town or
country, in Church or Chapel, for the erection or
reconstruction or drawing up specifications for new
ones, my Father was the sole authority.   Through
the organ builders of London and Bristol, his improvements and suggestions became adopted by
degrees ; and to the best of my knowledge brought
him oftentimes not even the credit of the invention.   It was a strange and true remark made to
me by the excellent Dr. Garrett of St. John's,
Cambridge, only a few years ago : " I had always
a mooning idea that in the matter of organs we
owed very much to your Father."   A mooning
idea ! Very suggestive simile ; conveying an idea
of extensive good, though you could not quite place,
nor define it.

" *Jan. 31st.*

" Amidst my troubles and complicated sorrows I have
commenced the composition of a Thanksgiving Anthem,
which I trust will prove a solace and comfort in my dis-
tress."

" *Feb, 11th.*

" Wellington came in the early part of the evening and
I had a couple of games of chess with him.   The fact was

that my head was by that time pretty well fagged, and
ached too, and my imagination was more disposed to
revert to ' Sehon, king of the Amorites and Og, the king
of Basan,' than to form chess combinations with facility.

" I read for a considerable time out of Matthew Henry's
Commentaries, but was more than ever impressed with
the conviction that such human labours rather tend to
impair than to exalt the effect of the perusal of the Bible,
excepting always such commentaries, and such only, as
have for their object the actual explanation or elucidation
of the text, the fixing of dates, &c., &c."

From his Monthly Review.

" February 29th.

" I have worked at my new Anthem *(Ps. 136)* very
slowly, and latterly the work has been altogether suspended by my bodily affliction. I am afraid that as a
whole it will turn out but poor disjointed stuff. It is to
conclude with a double fugue in eight real parts, a work of
no small labour, I ween.

" In the afternoon I took about ' forty winks ' of sleep,
and in the evening made a commencement of my fugue,
upon (with but trifling variation) the same subject which
I had thought of before I wrote a single bar of the
Anthem ! "

" March 7th.

" John Smith and I still disagree about the *tone* of the
Instrument (St. Stephen's Organ).   He almost insists
upon retaining the old and abominable *Wolf ;* instead of
distributing it throughout the system, throwing it into
glaring prominence in the Key of A♭."

" March 9th, 1835.

" John Smith called this morning and I gave him permission to cover the Swell-box of St. Stephen's organ

with box-boards instead of milled-boards, the former being perhaps in some respects even better adapted to the prevention of the transmission of sound than the latter, and 10 pr. cent. cheaper."

" March 22d.

" I made an attempt to bring the anthem to a conclusion, and think I now see my way clear to the doublebar."

" Never have I bestowed more labour on a composition than I have done on this ; and never perhaps felt less self-complacency on a review of the work when approaching its close."

And a few days before he says :

" My Fugue proceeded a little way.   It is a very heavy up-hill sort of a job."

" March 31st.

" I have contrived to finish my anthem *(Ps. 136)*, and T. H. Crook now has the Score to make a fair copy.

" Whether the composition be good for anything or not is more than doubtful.   Probably it is too elaborate."

" April 17th.

" I learnt to-day that a general invitation has been given to the whole of the Choral Society to attend and assist at the Opening of St. Stephen's Organ.

" At this rate I shall have a pretty mess of it !   'T will never do for me ! "

" April 19th.

" In the evening the church warden and one of the Vestry of St. Stephen's called here officially to request my undertaking the Opening of their new Organ, when we had a long discussion upon the proper mode of conducting that business.

" My notion and suggestion was that the most appro-

priate method was simply to get up a little quiet music
on the occasion in proper course, as forming part of the
regular church service, including an Anthem in the evening, and this course was ultimately resolved upon."

" May 3d.

" I went into town and spent much time at St. Stephen's.
The action of swell does not please me, being very unequal.
I begged Smith to try to improve it.

"At home at four.   I dined with Jubal.

" England tuned my Piano-forte this morning.   He
declined rendering any assistance on occasion of the
Opening of St. Stephen's Organ, on the ground that as a
Roman Catholic he could not join in the religious cere-
monies of any other ' sect.'

"I wish that all Protestants were as rigid!   Roman
Catholic Music in this country would then be at a very
low ebb."

A plan had been entertained of having a showy
performance, with additional vocalists and instru-
mentalists from Bath ; but my Father simply said
in that case he would withdraw ; whereupon his
plan and ideas were carried out.

By the 10th of May the weather had become
beautiful; his sufferings were well over, and his
notes were notes of thankfulness.   He writes,
" After nine hours of unbroken sleep I arose re-
freshed and gave God thanks."   His hours pass
rapidly in furthering his musical choir and organ
arrangements.   " Exhilarating mornings of glorious sunshine " succeed each other, and he says :

"I am thus picking up health by out-of-door exercise, and am truly thankful to my gracious Master for the improvement in that respect, of which I am conscious, and which my friends also have observed. 'T is wonderful too, considering the load of anxiety I have on my mind."

" May 11th.

"Before dinner I took Faustina and Handel a good walk through Clifton and the Hotwells. We witnessed the arrival of a good deal of shipping, the wind having veered round to the Westward. Home by four, after being absent two hours. Cold beef for dinner. Good meat and good appetite. In the evening we had a grand muster of vocalists and others, for a third rehearsal of the music for St. Stephen's. There were present twenty-four, including Handel (who led the second choir) and myself. We rehearsed nearly all the music that is to be done ; but there was toward the last some confusion owing to the frolicsomeness of three of the gentlemen aided by the sly humour of two others. All off by half past eleven.

"I was much fatigued, my patience having been worried in a very great degree. I did not go to bed for more than an hour later."

" May 13th.

"Another delightful morning. I spent it ' up in town ' in a very vagabondish manner, vibrating principally between St. Stephen's and certain printing offices in the vicinity. Soon after noon I ascended St. Stephen's Tower, in company with L. Livett and two other gentlemen. We there enjoyed the panoramic view of the city, and partook of bread and cheese and bottled porter!

"At half past six the grand Rehearsal took place at the Church.

"I sent for a fly and rode thither in company with a great quantity of music books. All the pieces, except my

ST. STEPHEN'S CHURCH, BRISTOL.

'Cantate' and 'Deus Misereatur,' were rehearsed. We did the Anthem thrice, and the Fugue yet once more. Still it was by no means *well* done. I hope and believe that all will go better on Sunday, when the parties will be inclined to conduct themselves decorously, if not devoutly. I was annoyed by some of them entering the Church and the Organ Gallery too, with their *hats* on. I placed Crook at the Organ to rehearse the 'Te Deum': he went on with the 'Jubilate' also. The organ answers very well, but requires the employment of its full power in accompanying nearly all the vocal music, otherwise the voices do not keep together."

" 14th.

"All the afternoon I was closely engaged writing out Psalm-tune Parts for my numerous choir of to-morrow; and at night I tried in vain to settle on a subject for an extempore voluntary to-morrow, but was obliged to go to bed without accomplishing the object."

" Sunday 15th.

"The service commenced precisely at eleven o'clock. The church was completely filled—aisles, chancel and all. Croft's 'This is the Day' went off with great spirit. I played a voluntary extempore, but was by no means happy in the effusion, and felt cramped by the limited nature of the Instrument. The Service (mine in C) went off trippingly, both morning and evening. The 'Kyrie' was particularly well sung, and the Psalm Tunes became (what they should be) genuine Chorales. The Anthem in the evening did not pass off as well as I could wish, some few of the points being either not taken up at all, or imperfectly executed. Had Handel been leader of the principal Choir, the whole would have gone off much better. For the postludes I took, in the morning 'The

Horse and his Rider,' Chorus of Handel ; in the evening, the Overture in 'Saul.'   For the Voluntary in the evening I played Bach's splendid Organ Pedal Fugue in G minor as a duet with Crook.   Neither of my Assistants however were sufficiently steady.

"The Chaunt in the evening was mine in G$^\sharp$ minor played in G$^\natural$, which was pronounced by Mr. Attwood, man-milliner and organist (!) to be one of the dullest things he ever heard ! "

" Sept 22d.

" I called at Christ Church and inspected the new organ in progress there.   Some of the Stops of the Choir and Swell are done ; but none as yet of the Great Organ. More of this instrument another time."

" Sept. 26th.

" I spent some time at Christ Church.   The Swell there on my new principle will be a fine one.   They have adopted also my Brass Pedals."

" Nov. 14th.

"I took Revs. John and Thomas West to Christ Church and there played the organ to them for a little while.   As the instrument approaches completion I do not like it as well as I thought I should.   Many of the arrangements are very awkward, clumsy, and ill-contrived. The Swell Pedal is out of the way and heavy in operation. The Pedals are too remote from the key-board and too far under the keys.   It is altogether a disagreeable instrument to play on, although the contents are upon the whole very good."

" Nov. 21st.

"Going through town I put in first at Christ Church (where the new organ approaches completion) and had a rattle upon the instrument."

" June 21, 1837.

" The official intelligence was this morning promulgated in Bristol that

" King William IV died yesterday at 2^h 12 A.M.

" Of course the bells tolled mournfully, but there was no grief.

" Concerning his short and inglorious reign I will say nothing here.   May the next be more prosperous."

" 23d.

" I endeavoured to select some words for a Funeral Anthem for the late King, and again failed ; I could find nothing appropriate."

" 26th.

" All the evening I was busy selecting words for a Funeral Anthem, or rather collecting words from which hereafter to make a selection.   They say the King is to be buried on the 6th of July.   If I do anything I must do it quickly."

" 29th.

" I came home and made an attempt at the opening recitation, etc., of an Anthem for William IV.   I worked until after midnight but did not make any very satisfactory progress."

" July 1st.

" I proceeded with the Anthem until nearly noon."

" July 4th.

" Before I went to bed I did a little (in pencil) at my Anthem, and finished it to-day."

" July 6th.

" King William IV. was buried this day at Windsor, but the Clergymen of Bristol were on this occasion too lazy to indulge their flocks with divine service on the day of interment, as they had done on the decease of former monarchs.

"The shops were shut; so were the churches and chapels. Of course therefore my new Anthem could not be publicly performed. Nevertheless I was bent upon launching my little composition after having taken the trouble to construct it, so I ordered some bills of the words to be printed (by Fuller, a radical, all the *tory* printers being full to overflowing of *election* work) at the foot of which I inserted the following memorandum:

"'Composed for the day of Interment, by Dr. Hodges; and now intended to be performed at St. James' Church, Bristol, *after the evening service,*
　　　　"'on Sunday July 9, 1837.'

"The bills to the number of one hundred and twelve only, were very nicely executed, and sent home in the evening.

"Meanwhile I ascended the hill and dined with my sister at Kingsdown Parade. In the evening I returned (about 8 o'clock,) picked up J. Birtill by the way, and held a second little partial rehearsal of the Anthem with him, Sam. Wallis, F. Hodges, and Handel.

"*Sunday, July 9th.*

"9.15 A.M., Domestic prayers. 10.30 I was at St. James,' and at 11 at St. Nicholas', where I distributed a few papers among particular friends.

"At 2.30, at my house in the Cloisters, we held another partial rehearsal of the Anthem.

"At 6 o'clock I was at St. James', and mustered up something like a choir. At the conclusion of the service there was a considerable augmentation of both the congregation and choir. I played the 'Dead March in Saul' and after a little delay we proceeded to perform my new Funeral Anthem for King William IV. The Anthem was got through pretty well. We could have added many more to the choir had we had copies wherewith to supply them. The audience was immense. The parson remained in the pulpit, the people remained in their pews. Crowds arrived from other places of worship. I hope they were gratified. All over, I came home to supper in peace and quietness."

The same year he wrote the following poem on Queen Victoria.

GOD SAVE THE QUEEN.

CHORAL GLEE.

Long life to our QUEEN!
The fairest e'er seen,
   And death to her foes,
   If such the world knows.
May a spotless renown
Attend on her Crown,
   And her glory extend
   Ever, world without end.

May peace and virtue never cease,
Through her long reign to find increase;
   And be VICTORIA'S name enrolled
On all our hearts—as on our gold.

Long life to our QUEEN!
The fairest e'er seen,
   And death to her foes,
   If such the world knows.
May a spotless renown
Attend on her Crown,
   And her glory extend
   Ever, world without end.

It was November 4, 1835, more than a year after the severe domestic affliction had befallen him, that he was invited to dine at the house of his learned friend, Dr. Alfred Day, and there to meet an American gentleman, the Rev. I. O. Choules.

He says : " The evening was spent very agreeably, principally in lively gossip about American manners, etc."

My Father's life then flowed on in its numerous channels, and on March 6 of 1836 he again met Mr. Choules, and says :

" We talked a little about my possible emigration to the United States. Choules said, that a man's sons constituted *Wealth* in that country."

The next day, according to promise, Mr. and Mrs. Choules visited my Father in his cloister study ; and the reader has only to fancy the old-time look of the large quaint room, with its artistic surroundings, and the host's genial, pleasant cordiality,—that freshness of youth mingled with the " old antiquary " suggestion of his dress and style, —to form a very pleasant picture. His own words give the interview best :

" I worked to-day at all available intervals at my Anthems, but actually *wrote in* nothing.

" Mr. Choules called by appointment about noon, and brought his wife with him. We now had a little discussion on the topic before alluded to, and he asked me, with evident seriousness, whether, if a good offer were made to me in America, I should be tempted to accept, and I replied most unhesitatingly in the affirmative. He undertook to bear the matter in mind, and said 'very probably I should receive a letter upon the subject, most likely from Dr. Wainwright.'

"I made up into a little parcel, ten copies of my 'Apology for Church Music,' for Choules, after inscribing three or four of them with the designations of certain influential and musical Clergymen, whom he named, including Dr. Wainwright aforesaid. Choules was begging books for a College Library now forming in the State of Maine, and I gave him 'Hume's Essay' and an anonymous 'Commentary on the Epistle to the Colossians.' Had we not been in such a hurry, I would have found him many more. His wife was particularly friendly, and both of them seemed much pleased with my old habitation. They remained here but a short time, and took a most affectionate leave. I believe that I shook hands with Mrs. C. no less than three times on her departure, viz., once in my study, (which Mr. C. said was the best study and most to his liking of any he had ever anywhere seen), once below stairs, and once more outside the house door."

And here of the good couple, we lose sight. Even this little characteristic, I might say *national*, friendliness of Mr. and Mrs. Choules may have had its effect on my Father and strengthened his inclination to the United States, although he did not at once decide to leave England.

Time again passes busily on with my Father, until

" *November 25, 1836.*

" At Smith's shop in Terrell Street, I heard casually, that Mr. Gray, of London, has just built a large organ for Boston, America. This led to an idea that possibly the Bostonians might make room for me as an Organist, and acting upon it, I wrote a letter of enquiry to Mr. Gray about it after my return home."

Mr. Gray after some days informed my Father that Dr. Wainwright was in England, and this resulted in my Father's meeting him at Portsmouth, where two or three conferences were held, which my Father says were " satisfactory " ; and he returns to Bristol in the "Celerity" coach, "which," he says, " was a very lazy one."

In his monthly retrospect my Father says :

" I have little doubt but that I shall receive a *call* to enter upon a new field of labour, on the other side of the Atlantic. I feel that I begin to set my heart upon this as the intended means of bringing my small talent into efficient exercise."

Another month passes, and in pessimistic vein perhaps, he writes :

" The taste of the age is carrying music into egregious folly. Everything now is done in an exaggerated manner. All old principles are uprooted and thrown aside. The vagaries of the *Opera* are to be brought into the *Church*. All system is to be exploded. Discord is to be exalted above concord, order and method are to be expunged, and our devotional melodies are to be constructed in subservience to the arch-demon of Reform. Sink or swin,—I cannot, I will not submit. If I continue in this my native country, it shall be one of my constant efforts to try to stem this torrent and to divert the public taste into the channel of common sense. On all hands it is confessed, that ecclesiastical music will not pay, and in composition I am doing just nothing at all.

"Even now a winged messenger may be on his way across the mighty deep to beckon me to the American shore. *There*, I shall start in a new scene, with new vigour, new views, new encouragement, and what would be newest of all, every prospect of benefitting others and reaping a comfortable revenue for myself."

Again his active life goes on, and on the 17th May, my Father receives a letter from Dr. Wainwright, which, although conveying no definite offer, speaks very confidently of his success in the event of his resolving to cross the water. He refers him for further information to a Mr. Mason, by whom he (Dr. W.) had sent a letter, and couples an invitation to visit Boston with the offer of hospitality at his own house. Finally, he says that he is about to get up some of my Father's music at his own Church, and hopes to hear from him soon again.

"*May 24th.*

" On this day the Princess Victoria, Heiress presumptive to the Throne of these realms, became of Royal age (eighteen years), and bells were rung in Bristol, but there was no general holiday.

" I began writing to Dr. Wainwright yesterday. I wrote to Mr. Lowell Mason, inviting him to Bristol."

And in his closing review of the month, he says :

" Two flattering letters have just at this critical period arrived from Dr. Wainwright, encouraging my idea of Emigration to the United States. I have since, however, corresponded with his friend, Lowell Mason, now in London, who does not appear quite so sanguine of my chance of emolument in Boston or New York as the Doctor.

" America, too, happens to be in a state of fearful commercial embarrassment, and all things considered, I have resolved to postpone for a time the project of expatriation and to try once more to effect a comfortable settlement in my beloved native country."

The last weeks in our old Cloister home passed in a kind of sad, confused dream, as though some dreaded event impended. Our Father seemed already removed from us in purpose and occupation—but doubly near us in anxiety and sympathy. I shall never forget the portending look of the large trunks in his study and the preparations being made for a journey to Canada, as well as a voyage to New York, in those days points of tremendous distance.

That which I remember very distinctly was his own individual character, which so impressed itself upon me, viz. : his marvellously strong and unwavering purpose, his rapid, nervous action, his suppression of every feeling that might have caused himself pain or encouraged sorrow in us, his great influence on all around him and their confidence in

RESIDENCE OF DR. HODGES IN THE CLOISTERS, BRISTOL.

his strength and judgment (for many friends were
there to carry on his wishes and see to final arrangements), and the courage with which he went bravely
working on and cheering us by his spirit and
energy.

The last day came,—the carriage was at the door,
and the last piece of luggage put upon it.

With amazing calmness and courage he summoned all the household around him in our usual
sitting room.   He took his seat at the table ; *behind*
him above the mantel, was the great carved shield
which had on it these words, in his splendid large
writing :

" Omnia Vanitas."

True enough it was of worldly things ; but *before*
him lay his large Bible, which he opened at the
46th Psalm, and from this indeed there came a different voice.   Silence fell on us all, and we watched
his face with a sense of awe, as he proceeded to
read in firm tones, yet with evident and deep emotion, the *Deus Noster Refugium*, the old Festeburg
of Luther.   Each verse of this noble burst of sublime trust of the Hebrew Monarch came out with
a power unknown to us before.   It seemed to be
pointing out, as he meant it to be, both to himself
and to us all, in this sore trial and for all our lives,
a veritable Refuge and Strength.

7

Many a cloud have I passed under since that day, many a struggle for strength has been gone through, many a prayer for help been uttered, many an hour have I endured when the " chilling rain " made " life seem never the same again "; but the deep impression of that scene of my childhood in the old Cloister home can never fade away; and again I see my Father's inspired face, as in his sorrow and great trust he read the grand words,

" The Lord of Hosts is with us, the God of Jacob is our Refuge."

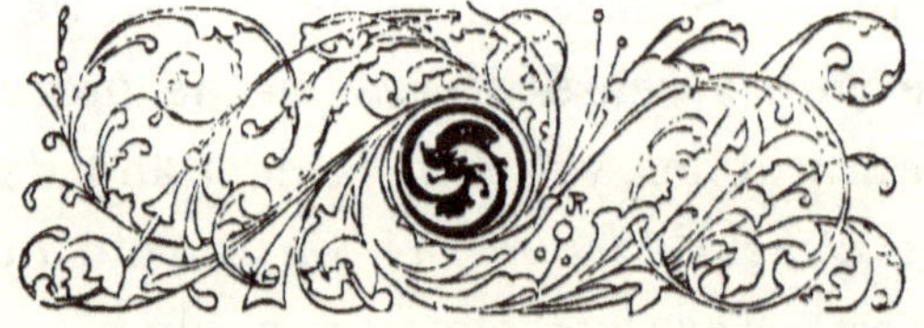

CHAPTER VIII.

TEMPORA MUTANTUR.

IT is in Bristol in the fall of the year 1838, and
the Cathedral service is just over. Two
ladies, who have come in late, evidently in travelling costume, and have enjoyed the service from
the transept, stand awhile listening to the last
" Amen," lost in thought in the significant silence
which follows it. They listen also to the Voluntary,
and then follow the white-robed procession into the
cloisters. They seem to be strangers, yet evidently acquainted with the place. They pass the
Norman pillars before the Chapter Room, and the
Churchyard gate and the Bishop's Palace door, and
soon stand before the now deserted looking Eliza-
bethan house, missing from the central door the
brass plate on which was engraved in pretty large
letters, DR. HODGES.

They ring, and they knock with the great, old-
fashioned, circular, black knocker.

No answer.

One of the old Cathedral vergers, seeing them,

comes forward, and in answer to their questions, informs them that the Doctor has " gone to America, taking with him his oldest boy, ' Master Handel '; that the two daughters are up at Kingsdown, at Miss West's school."

" And the little boys ? "

" They are at Dr. Day's School, Ma'am, and the *very little* one is well cared for until he is old enough to go there too."

The pleasant, English face of the honest old verger lighted up as he went on.

" A sore loss to us all, Ma'am, is the Doctor. It don't seem right that he had to leave us. He was always right pleasant, and had a cheery word and a joke for us always ; and many 's the good kind deeds he did when he heard any one was in trouble. He would take long walks and put himself out to help them. There was nights, Ma'am, when the cloisters seemed *full* of music, such grand singing ! and all from his study window up yonder. There was one kind of music he did not like himself, and that was the old *organ grinders ;* and as sure as ever they got themselves and their monkeys inside the gates and begun grinding their old hurdy-gurdy, out would come some one from the Doctor's with a sixpence for them to ' be off.' Ah ! we 've had a loss, and Bristol too ; for every one seemed to know him, and a kindlier gentleman never walked the streets o' Bristol. And the scholars, too, was after him; but 't was not for that he was so much thought of.

"I used to think myself, Ma'am, that he had some trouble on his mind at times, as he would walk to and fro, up and down, in the cloisters there oftentimes till after nightfall. Maybe he was thinking his music. We all knew that he was a great musician and the music we heard from that window up there was his own writing out. Yes, 't is a big loss for us all. The cloisters don't seem the same without him, and Mr. Handel too! As full of mischief as ever a boy was, was he! I mind the time when he and other boys with him clambered the high wall and was over in a jiffy into the Bishop's garden, and there they was robbing the pear tree like fun. 'Old Phillips' got wind of it and went quick to the garden, as those was his favourite pears—and was just in time to catch one boy up the tree; but Mr. Handel—nobody could ever catch him! He made for the old ruins, and there he hid away; and old Phillips came along to the cloisters with one big boy by the collar, and poor little Mr. Jubal who was crying for fright about his brother. He was too gentle and too little to have gone in with these boys. Mr. Handel, he came in as

right as could be, with the pears in his pocket, and
the big boy got out of the window where he was
shut up in Phillips' house, and made off fast on his
legs.

"A mighty mischievous boy was Mr. Handel,
and beautiful too, and how he did sing ! that voice
of his ! no matter if the Doctor had a hundred
singers, Mr. Handel's voice would clear them all ;
so sweet and strong it was.

"The Doctor had some sad times here too,
Ma'am. He 'most broke his heart for his little
Deborah, when she died, and was carried from here
to St. Maryport Churchyard. There was another
too, but she was but a little baby when she died,
and did not know him, and trot after him as Deborah did. Her name was Cecilia. Deborah never
minded what he did to her. When she heard his
knock and ring, she would run to the door, and he
would tuck her up like a bundle under his arm, and
carry her along, she laughing like everything.

"And it is but like as tho' yesterday that the
Cathedral bell was tolled for Mrs. Hodges ; a lovely
lady was she, and so young to go, and leave her
family, and the little weeny boy but a month old !
'T was a sad October day that ! The black coaches
and the hearse was a sorrowful sight to see in the
cloisters, and sadder yet to see the poor Doctor

and his three boys all in the long black cloaks and hat-bands. That is just three years since.

" Mrs. Hodges was a wonderful singer too, and before her illness came on, her voice went clear and strong over all the rest, just as Mr. Handel's did after her.

" He was a wonderful boy at the organ too, and has, for now eighteen months past, helped the Doctor when Mr. Crook went to St. Michael's ; and small as he is, there he would sit at the big organ at St. James', or at St. Nicholas', and go right through the service. Well, Ma'am, I must spare telling you more, but we 've all had a great loss. Every one who knew the Doctor loved him. There never was a poor person he knew wanted, but in many ways, not only in money, he would try to help him. I have known him have to borrow a little at Church if he had seen some one suffering, when he gave all the change he had. They 'll get a good man and a great musician too over the sea in New York, and we have lost him ; but we can't forget him here at home."

The verger left and the ladies gave a parting look at the walled-in Norman arch at the end of the house, above which were bunches of snap-dragons and wall-flowers growing, and the tendrils of a vine hanging down. Then they passed the cloister gates, and turning down the "Lower Green," surveyed the perfect Norman arch, built over with stuccoed houses.

" This must have been one great entrance to the Monastery ; and this was the way to the Bishop's Garden, south of the Doctor's premises."

They found their way in ; and saw the ruins of the Bishop's Palace, which ran out in a southerly direction, dividing the large garden. " I do not wonder Dr. Hodges chose this old place," said one, " it has a charm of its own."

" Just see those immense walls ! The Doctor told me that some in *his* house are three feet thick, and that both the Palace and his house are built on a Norman substructure of low arches, such as you see in crypts. Just see that lovely Gothic window of the palace, and how the kind ivy has draped it ! They say the eastern side is lovely with terraced gardens and steps, and up to the left, the really fine south-eastern end of the Cathedral in full view ! No doubt these houses were built over the destroyed Monastery, when Henry VIII. converted Bristol into a See."

They hurried out, and turned up to the " Prior's Lodge," where they stood admiring that interesting and picturesque dwelling.

" *This* was Dr. Hodges' poetic dream of a house ! Every stone of it speaks of him. Gothic window,

NORMAN GATEWAY, BRISTOL CATHEDRAL.

music-room, study window, do you see how beautiful it is? And the ivy-hidden one above? and his garden and trees? Then, what a very unique and *unlike-other-people* look and way he had with him ! Oh, it is all charming ! As if he belonged to just such a place ! So close to this grand Arch, too, ' The Monastery Gateway' and the Cathedral Tower behind! Hark, there is the Quarter-bell ! Let us wander round and close our ramblings in the Abbey Church, thankful that amid the destruction that fell on so many magnificent Christian Churches in this our little island, *ours* was at least partially spared. Perhaps the former Nave reached to this very spot ! "

Then they went into the Cloister again and entered as the bell struck the " ninth hour—the hour of prayer." Mutilated as was the Cathedral, it was still solemn and imposing. The sweet organ-tones of the Stopped Diapason were penetrating and almost singing as the procession passed in. The matchless service went on, with its plaintive monotone, and sweet harmonies of the preces and versicles. Then came the Psalms, that unequalled part of the service in the hands of this Organist, the true antiphon of the melodious double chant, floating and echoing away ; the taste and fancy of the player all called out as he varied from swell and solo, choir and pedals, according to the words ;

all the voices of song blending in one fascinating whole. There was no set *Service* sung, nor was the Anthem in any way remarkable ; and when the beautiful evening prayers were said, and the last " Amen " sung, our two friends went out, the very last of the congregation, at the northern door into the Green, and the verger locked it after them.

The foregoing is partly imaginary, partly fact, indeed, *all* fact with imaginary speakers.

The Bishop's Palace was burnt at the Bristol Riots in October, 1831, and has never been re-built.

The Cathedral has a mural tablet to the memory of William Phillips, the subsacrist, for his bravery in defending the Cathedral door against the rioters.

The interest and knowledge of our family shown by the verger are not at all out of the common. The men belonging to a Cathedral remain long there, and become attached to those living in the precincts. As children, the good old men were like friends to us. We used to love to go in when they opened the Cathedral to ring the quarter-bells. Their gowns, and kind old faces, and attitudes, as with one foot in the noose, they pulled regularly at the ropes, all were fascinating. We always went back to our house when the " College boys " (and hour of service) approached.

CHAPTER IX.

MY Father was accompanied to America by his eldest and brilliant son, George F. Handel, without whom it does not seem possible that he could have gone. On their journey to Liverpool they were met at a Midland station by the Rev. Mr. Havergal and his daughter, Miriam, for a few parting words, Miriam bringing my Father a beautiful bunch of flowers.

They sailed on the New York Packet *Sheridan*, leaving Liverpool early in August, and arriving in New York, on their way to Canada, early in September. My Father had received the appointment of Organist to the Cathedral of St. James at Toronto, but on his arrival there he found the city in so disturbed a state that he was obliged to give up the idea of remaining there, and accepted the call to Trinity Church, New York.

On the voyage my Father gave way to the usual cheerfulness of his disposition which, when with others, never forsook him. His readiness of wit, his marvellous power of adaptation to circumstances, his quick sympathies and happy sociality, no doubt here had free play. He never regarded any one as a stranger. Behind every human face he knew there was a human heart ; and he had a larger one himself than most. The benignant gladness of his spirit was always ready to enliven a passing social hour ; and the following verse shows a vein of fun coursing through his mental structure, one which was never ascetic or austere :

" Said Maurice to Daniel one day after dinner,
' How strangely you lick up your wine, you old sinner ;
Every minute you 're lifting your glass from the table,
Repeating potations as fast as you 're able.'
' I do no such thing,' replied Dan in a passion ;
' De'il take me if ever I swallow that fashion.'
' Avast with your rage,' then cried Maurice to merry
　　Dan,
No longer swig claret, but always drink sherry, Dan ! ' "

The following extracts from the graphic and affectionate letters of my brother, George F. Handel, to his sisters, written in all the natural freshness of boyhood and under the exhilaration of new scenes in a new country, throw light on my Father's life at that time. Much that shows the versatility of my brother's character has to be omitted ; but the one vein running through them all is his intense and thorough-going devotion to his father. He was one with him in his position, his feelings, his progress, and his prospects ; entering into his life with an admiration and reverence for his person, as rare as it was beautiful, and united to a feeling of almost brotherly sympathy.

Amid the deprivations and difficulties which my Father encountered during these early years of his life in New York, the companionship and musical intelligence of this loving son must have been an inexpressible comfort to him. The sunshine of his presence and his numerous talents, especially for the organ, will not soon be forgotten. I have listened to warm mention of them as late as 1894. A beautiful painting of his yet more beautiful face, by Stephen Hague, grandson of a former Professor of Cambridge, is still preserved.

The first glimpse we catch of my Father and brother in the New World is in a letter dated

"Toronto, Canada, Sept. 24, 1838.

" We sent on our heavy baggage to Toronto, and followed ourselves, on the 10th, for Albany, 151 miles, at seven in the morning. Got there at 6 P.M.

" The steamer, that we came in is a nasty, ricketty old thing, ten years old. She has four chimneys and four boilers, with two engines on deck ; (as all the Yankee steamers have.) We slept at Albany and proceeded for

Utica at eight next morning by the Railroad. You never saw such a wilderness as it runs through! We had in our train twenty-one coaches besides the baggage cars, all crammed with passengers, the longest train they ever had.

"In consequence of the length and having only one engine, we did not get to Utica till three hours after the time.

"It is ninety-six miles from Albany and we were eight hours doing it.

"We took a Canal Boat (a line boat,—the packet boats were all full) immediately; but they had more than forty passengers. We were obliged to have each meal three times (served), the cabin was so small; also we were obliged to sleep in the Baggage Room on the baggage.

"Arrived at Syracuse at 6 P.M., Sep. 12. 308 miles from New York. Slept at the Hotel; took our place in a Packet Boat (not a steam packet) for Oswego, sixty miles. The Boat was to start at 10 A.M. but did not till 3 P.M. We were in a delightful state of suspension, but not at all impatient, as you may imagine. Arrived at Oswego at one in the morning. Slept till five o'clock with our clothes on, and then we turned out to look for a steamer for Toronto, but were disappointed. So we took places for Kingston in the *Great Britain* Steamer (English colours once more) and got there at one, having started at eight, 67 miles. I should imagine myself on the Atlantic for all that I could see. There was no steamer for Toronto till midnight, so we went on board to bed at 10 o'clock. At 2 P.M., we started for Toronto and arrived there safely at 8½ P.M. Sep. 15.

"Papa left me on board while he went to look for the Archdeacon, got to the 'North American Hotel' where we still are; but I must tell you more in my next. I have to pay (at least my father has) 1/10½ *d.* on each letter, so Papa says, I must not write too many. Most likely I shall get into the ' Iron and General Hardware Business.' The Archdeacon has called two or three times about it. But Messrs. Ridout Brs. & Co. were out."

"*New York, Nov. 10th, 1838.*

" You will no doubt be surprised when you see where we are, but not when I tell you the reason. The times were so bad, business so dull, everything so stagnant in the way of work, that Papa made up his mind not to stay any longer.

" We accordingly left in the Steamer *William IV* at 12 o'clock on Saturday morning, purposing to go to Oswego, but it was so rough we were obliged to put into Kingston on Sunday morning. We staid there till Monday morning, 5 o'clock, when we got on board the *United States.*

" Arrived at Oswego in the afternoon, slept there, and proceeded next morning by Canal Boat to Utica, got there Wednesday morning at 8, took the nine o'clock train for Albany and got there at four the same afternoon. From Albany we came to New York in the Steamer *North America* and safely landed in New York once more at 6 o'clock Thursday morning.

" The same morning, Papa found me a place as one of the clerks to John Delafield, Esq., who is about to establish a new Banking Company in New York. I sleep and board at his house.

" I must now tell you about Canada, which is again in trouble. The Rebellion broke out the day we left, so we got out of it in time. The Government have chartered two steamboats, the *Traveller* and *Queen Victoria* and have ordered the English steam boats not to touch at any American Ports on the Lake. Two of the State prisoners broke out of jail at Montreal, and have since returned with about 2,000 rebels. One day in Toronto a gentleman lent me his horse, and I rode three or four miles up George St. and saw the place where the battle of Montgomeries' Hill was fought last winter. There are all the ruins of houses burnt down by the rebels there yet, and it looks like a wilderness. It seemed to me just like leaving home again coming away from Toronto; I had got acquainted with so many people there. There is a great difference in the style of beauty here and in Toronto. Here the ladies screw up their waists to almost nothing.

"The winter had begun in Canada before we left. Snow was three or four inches on the ground, and ice was thick. When we got to New York it was raining and the weather was too warm for a great coat; while in Canada we were glad to put on two or three, or else sit by the stove. New York in one respect looks more like England than Canada does, *viz.*, in the burning of coal instead of wood. We did not see one coal fire while in Canada.

"The steamboats are very safe about New York, but down in Mississippi they blow them up ' like everything.' A steamer will not last more than a twelve-month, and then it is either blown up by accident (*par accident tou-jours*) or wrecked going down that immense river. Address your letter to me or to Papa at Dr. Wainwright's, to whose house Papa has removed."

My Father was made Director of the Music of Trinity Parish in February, 1839.

" February 22nd, 1839.

"I go to St. John's Church in St. John's Park, or Hudson Square. I go with Mr. and Mrs. Delafield, but do not sit in their pew since Papa has been organist."

The following letters give us an insight into my Father's earliest work in Trinity Parish :

"*April 17th, 1839.*

" One choir consists of six paid persons and one supernumerary, G. F. H. Hodges, by name, I generally being an attendant in the organ gallery, in which Dr. Hodges presides. Our music is very good, and, with a little more practice, will get better. We sing a 'Te Deum' and 'Jubilate' every Sunday, and that is more than you do in your churches ; also, there is 'playing in' and 'playing out'; and some bad boys and girls on each side of the organ play all through the service. The first Sunday, we sang 'E. H. in F,' the second Sunday, 'Boyce in C,' and the third and fourth, 'Hodges in F' again. (This is a great favourite this side of the water.) We have sung 'Jackson in E' twice, and 'Boyce in C' again. This Service is considered rather heavy and does not go down very well, although we sing it as well as any other. On Palm Sunday, we sang the 'Benedicite' to a chaunt,— Easter Sunday, 'playing in' full organ : 'Christ our Passover' to a chaunt of Battishill, 'Gloria Patri' after *last* Psalm, 'Te Deum,' 'Boyce in A,' (not liked so well as 'E. H. in F' or 'Jackson in E') 'Jubilate' Do. Easter Hymn to Dr. Worgan's Tune, and before sermon a Psalm (metrical) to Papa's tune 'Benevolence.' Before the Communion, an anthem ; Recitative Bass, Quartet and Chorus, by Jas. Corfe (requested by Dr. Wainwright).

" Next Sunday, Papa's Service in C, a great favourite, and next 'Boyce in A' again. This is for the twelfth time of asking. If any of you know just cause or impediment that side of the water, why Dr. Hodges and his choir should not sing 'Te Deum,' etc., etc., on this side of the water, as well (if not better) than you do on that side of the water, ye are all herewith and hereby, in-

vited to come to this side of the water and hear for
yourselves.

"I remain your affectionate brother,
                    "George F. H. H.,
                        "on this side of the pool."

"*June 8th.*

"This week has been an important week in relation to
our music, but Papa will, I doubt not, write to some one
and tell it better than I can, as he knows more of it. We
are restricted to two stops, all the rest being too loud.

"I played this afternoon, as Papa was too unwell and
too melancholy to come to church and be tied down to
such narrow compass.

"I only used two stops at the same time, and they only
in the Choir or Swell; and only one stop when I played
on the Great Organ. Papa will no doubt give you some
of the news. He has written to Thos. Crook. We hope
he gets on well at Clifton Church and St. James."

"*Sept. 13th.*

"My business at the Bank goes on very briskly, I like
it very well. I get through there by 4½ to 5 o'clock.
Then I generally go and see Papa; and if he is at home,
I sit a little while with him, and if we feel inclined, we
play a game of chess. If he is out or busy, I go to Mr.
Delafield's house in town and practice on the Piano.
Sometimes I get up at six in the morning and go and
practice there.

"To-morrow I move to No. 70 Franklin St. and Papa
moves in a day or two afterwards to the same house. He
will have a larger room and will have his Piano. I suppose
I shall not practice much on it except when he goes out,
and then I shall get down there and practice away 'like
everything,' as they say sometimes in New York. I wish

you would give me some news of the Cloisters ; whether they are going to re-build the Bishop's Palace.

" I have played for Papa several times at church.

" I saw the *British Queen* and the *Great Western* both together the last time the former was here. The *British Queen* is a great deal the largest, but I do not think she is near so good a model as the *Great Western*

" Papa has gone into the State of New Jersey with a gentleman to spend the day. To-morrow, I believe he goes to Boston to meet Dr. Wainwright. The ladies screw in their waists and dress most extravagantly. There is no city where they pay more attention to dress than New York, except perhaps New Orleans."

" March 12th, 1840.

" MY DEAREST FAUSTINA:

" It was with great pleasure that on last Saturday, I heard that the *Great Western* was telegraphed at eleven o'clock as being in the Lower Bay.

" At 12 o'clock, I ran round to the Battery, and was just in time, for she was about half a mile off when I got there ; and, although she had only been telegraphed an hour, yet the Battery was thronged with persons to witness her arrival. It was blowing a perfect hurricane at the time ; the water was at its height, and it looked like a little sea. The waves beat on the Wall of Walks, so that no one could go nearer than about twelve feet from the edge. There were two sloops at anchor, and beating against the wall, but we did not look at them. All eyes were directed towards the magnificent steamer bowling up, end on, with all flags hoisted, and leaning gently over to the wind, every now and then firing a big gun. When she got up to the Battery, she stopped her paddles, and gently glided up the East River to her dock, foot of Clinton Street. I almost shed tears at the sight, and I believe that if any one had hullo'd (softly !) in my ear at

the time I should not have heard it, so intent was I on
the ship in question.   I thought to myself, ' what news
does she bring?   Good or bad ; forty-two days later from
England !   A great deal of good or evil might have happened in that time, almost four months since I have heard
from my dear Brothers and Sisters.'   Such were my
thoughts at sight of the *Great Western.*"

"*March 12th.*

" Papa and I play chess very often of an evening, but
he beats me rather shamefully, though he has a great deal
more trouble, as I do sometimes get a game now with all
the pieces on.   And at home he could beat me with a
Queen and two Castles off."

"*May 5th.*

" Our new organ at St. John's Church is almost finished, and the people are much pleased, delighted,
charmed and edified with it.   Papa is quite well, though
he was very ill for two or three days, about three weeks
ago.   I am sending a *Commercial Advertiser.*   It contains
a paragraph referring to one of us !   Papa has been playing over some of his old favorites, J. S. Bach's ' Fugues,'
and is now gone out for a little while."

" We have a very pretty little Tortoise shell kitten,
which occupies a great deal of my spare time after tea.
She is the *dearest* little cat I ever saw, not excepting your
old tom (can't even afford a capital t).   This evening Papa
and I have been playing chess, and talking over the news
by the *President*, and I put the little cat into the chess
box, where she staid very good and quiet for two hours
and a half, without attempting to get out.   Sometimes
she would put her little head out over the top and look
at our men.   When we called ' check ' she would start ;
but the greater part of the time she was snuggled down
to sleep.   She just filled Papa's old chess box ; at all
events, he never had a larger animal in it."

"May 7th.

" Last Sunday I played at St. Paul's Church, morning and afternoon. This is my first appearance in this quarter. The late organist has left, and as some of the Music Committee are out of town, Papa sends me to play until they make an appointment. It is not by any means a fine organ, except as regards the tone of some of the stops. There are no Pedal pipes. Papa has a very fine one at St. John's Church, which will be completed in about a fortnight. It is certainly a very fine instrument, and will be the best in the city, probably in the country."

"New York, June 21st.

" I am at present Deputy Organist, under Papa, of St. Paul's Church. This morning (Sunday) I proceeded at 10 o'clock precisely out of the front door and was on my way to St. Paul's, which I reached in safety, and began playing the Parson and persons in at 10½, our old St. James' time, you see! (U. C!) There is a pretty good choir and we get along pretty well; only since the first week in May have I played there. The organ is no great shakes, though I make some great shakes upon it occasionally. It is an old one built by G. P. England, London. There are no pedals, and each rank of keys is separate and distinct from the other, and incapable of coupling or combining.

" Papa has just sounded his call for me on the piano. So I leave this 'till a more convenient season.'"

"New York, Nov. 30th.

" I sent you a newspaper called the Albion by the President, S. S. It contains a favourable mention of Papa, which I dare say you have discovered. I bought ever so many, and sent them to different friends in England, and in this country. Papa played the organ at Mr. and Mrs. Wood's first Sacred Concert, which I think was the cause of the article.

"We had an exhibition of the organ at St. John's, of which I will talk in Miriam's letter.

"I still play at St. Paul's Church. Papa told me at dinner that he had heard my playing on Sunday evening spoken highly of. Hurrah! I cannot write more as I want to practice on my piano. Good-night!"

"Dec. 1st.

"MY DEAREST MIRIAM:

"Last Friday evening, we had virtually, a Sacred Concert; though nominally, an Exhibition of the new Organ at St. John's Chapel, where Papa is organist.

"I went round to the church a little before half-past five and found everything right, a man lighting the lamps, and another putting the Programmes in the pews. I took about six or eight of these to Mr. Delafield's, to show and give them to Mr. and Mrs. D., as I expected the church would be crowded and they would hardly have a chance to get any. Mr. D. told me he was going to send his coachman to secure his pew for him so that they might be sure of a good seat, his being in a very central position. I then went home to tea, and went to the church again at 7 o'clock.

"It was then almost full, and the people were pouring in from the North and from the South, from the East and from the West.

"I ran home for a lady who had volunteered her services to help on this occasion. I seated her comfortably in the organ gallery and left her peeping through the curtain at some gentlemen, to go on my voyage of discovery through the church. I found Mr. and Mrs. D. in a strange pew, for although they had sent their coachman an hour and a half before the time, yet their pew was filled, and as the church was open to all, every pew was free. I had a small conversation with them and also with Harriot D., who was some pews behind them. I thought I would go up the middle aisle to see the organ and how it looked, and was in danger of being left there, for I could, with difficulty, get to the door as the people were pouring in so fast; this was about twenty minutes before the time. While engaged in the charitable work of trying to get seats for some pretty girls and an old gentleman, the clock struck seven. I hurried to get back again, but the people, —who were now so thick that I could have walked on their heads all over the church—kept crowding and pushing so that it took me several minutes of hard work to get back to the organ gallery. I was almost going to give it up as a bad job, but persevered till I gained my end.

" I sent you a *Herald* which you will receive before this and which will give you an account of the performances; and also contains a high compliment to Papa. So much for that. I have a Piano and last night I played ' Home sweet home!' upon it.

"Your truly affectionate Brother,

HANDEL."

" *April 30th, 1841.*

" I went last evening to attend Rehearsal of the choir at St. John's School-room. As it rained hard, only one or two, including the organists, came. I wish you could have seen Papa last night, wrapped up in his Macintosh, (that funny check one), overshoes, and that green umbrella and hat extra-ordinary. Do you think you would have known him? Nevertheless, he looked natural to me, that 's flat. But I tell you he looked sharp at me, when I entered, for he did not expect me."

My Brother had ruptured a small blood vessel. He tried to prevent his Father's anxiety on his account.

" New York, May 1st, 1841.

" I continue to play the organ as Papa's Deputy at St. Paul's Church, and occasionally encounter some stray incidents. I will, if I can remember, repeat one.

" One Sunday evening, I was warming myself by the fire before commencement of the service. Papa was in the vestry, or else had not come, I forget which. I was suddenly accosted after this manner by a thick-set, ugly-looking, what-once-had-been-red-haired man, a non-official but very officious member of the church :—

" ' Mr. Hodges, we have heard that your Father is going back to England and were in hopes that you are going too, for we don't like your music at all.' Here a long conversation ensued, which left no new principle settled, and was only stopped by the bell announcing it $7\frac{1}{2}$ o'clock, when I ran up to the organ, opened the door, and began playing. We might have gone on with our conversation to this day but for that bell. O, Miriam ! We have had such grumbling, such fault-finding and such unpleasant speeches made in this church within the last twelve-month that it has been a very unpleasant berth.

" The same thing has been gone through at St. John's and they have made up their minds to it ; so I suppose we cannot expect a like reform in a shorter space, especially when there are so many old folks."

" Sunday Morning, June 13th, 1841, Hellgate.

" My Dear Brothers and Sisters :

" Being out of town as you see by the date, and it being a wet morning, and as we are deprived of the privilege of going to church, the best thing I can do is to write a general letter to you all. How sorry we are to hear of poor dear Miriam's illness ! What a trial it is !

NORMAN ARCH, IN COLLEGE GREEN, BRISTOL.

Let us all *hope* for the best, and at the same time be prepared for the worst. 'We know not what a day may bring forth.'

"I have not been well at all this winter, having been troubled with a severe cough. Seeing that I had got very thin and lost all my colour, Mr. and Mrs. Delafield kindly invited me to their cottage, whither I come every afternoon after bank hours. Papa has procured some one to play for me at St. Paul's this morning.

"I enjoy myself greatly out here and feel greatly benefited. The weather has been very warm for the last three weeks, having attained to 93 degrees at times, but yesterday the wind got round to the northeast and we have a cold rain. I am now sitting in an old green-house, which Mr. Delafield has altered, having put a floor to it even with the parlours, and made it into a very pretty little sitting-room.

"The tide is just coming up, and vessels are passing both ways.

"The air is delightful, it has just ceased raining, though the sun has not yet made its appearance, and it is a question whether it will to-day.

"The flowers and garden generally look much improved; the birds are singing delightfully; the tree-toads now and then croaking; the katydids have not yet made their appearance. Moschetos are very plentiful and my hands, face, etc., suffer from their mischievous bites.

"I read Jubal's letter to Papa to Mrs. Delafield. We had several very hearty laughs over it. Where does he get all his big words from? Mrs. D. wants him to write an 'elaborate account' of what he finds in America, should he ever visit it; what he thinks of the people, indeed she wants an 'elaborate account' of his *thoughts* on America and the Americans. She also expressed a desire to see his Journal of his Voyage, and all his thoughts that he writes down. Would it not be amusing? Yes, ' I guess ' it would.

"My love to all dear friends.

"Your affectionate brother,

"HANDEL."

CHAPTER X.

ON the 11th of April, 1844, the organ of St. Paul's Chapel, New York, gave forth its most jubilant sound, as a small party turning from the altar, proceeded down the middle aisle to the Broadway gate. The player was my Father's faithful disciple, John F. Huntington, who surprised him by thus announcing the happy marriage of Dr. Edward Hodges to Miss S. A. Moore, of New York. The ceremony was performed by the Right Rev. Benjamin T. Onderdonk, D.D., Bishop of New York.

My second mother, Miss Sarah Ann Moore, was one of the most charming and agreeable women in the large and refined circle in which she moved. Sparkling and fascinating in conversation, unostentatious and natural in manner, it was impossible for her not to attract all in the intellectual society, which gathered around her brother, Nathaniel F. Moore, LL.D., who at the time of her marriage, was Greek Professor and afterwards, President of Columbia College, New York. Among the intellectual she had a right to move, being the daughter of a distinguished physician, the niece of Bishop Moore of New York, and first cousin of Clement C. Moore, LL.D., Hebrew Professor at the General Theological Seminary, New York. She spoke French and Italian with fluency and ease, her preceptor in the latter language having been Signor Daponte, who had arranged the Libretto of Don Giovanni for Mozart ; and she numbered literary men of England, Italy, and France amongst her friends.

During one of her visits abroad her bust was taken by Thorwaldsen ; and in New York she had received vocal lessons of Madame Malibran. Naturally fond of music and highly cultivated in opera and other branches of the study, sacred music of a high order, and the school of our Cathedral composers were quite unknown to her. The services she had heard while in England had not reached her heart. Thus she was the more ready to acknowledge in my Father a Master in the Sacred Art ; and devotedly true to this she remained to the end of her life. She was attracted curiously by his appearance and his dress ; and used laughingly to tell the story of her first meeting him at her cousin, Dr. Clement Moore's gate. On asking Dr. Moore who that was, he replied : " Why, Sarah, that is the great Dr. Hodges !" " Dear me," she said, " I thought it was an old Scotch peddler !" When married to him she called him her " old English pedaler." Another title she gave him was, " The ineffable Hodges," as she loved " Hodges in F." more than any other service he used. Unaccustomed to the highest form of German music, she used to exclaim as she heard my Father's daily rendering of one or two of Sebastian Bach's ' Fugues,' " Oh those horrid Fugues !" But gradually and surely her tone changed. She began to like, and then to *love* them ; and on no account would miss " the Doctor's morning ' Fugue.'"

She was very clever at extemporary versification, but withal her character shone brightest in the daily round of her life. She was beloved by all classes ; rich and poor, the scholarly and the humble. She could hear of no case of sickness or sorrow without doing her utmost to relieve it. A perfect sincerity governed speech and action ; she was exactly the same whether adorning a literary circle, or reading the Bible at the bedside of one of her humble poor. She was generous in spirit, faithful and loving in every relation of life. Perhaps her most beautiful characteristic was the zeal

and entirety with which she entered into my
Father's life.   With her practical mind she blended
a high and religious ideal.   Her spirit was recep-
tive to a great degree, and was capable of great
exaltation through sacred music.

From the first she perceived, acknowledged, and
almost worshipped the gift that was in my Father.
This it was that united them in this world ; and
may we not hope that this " Blest tie that binds,"
is extended to a deeper, holier, loftier bliss, in the
" Realm of Perfect Accord."

We will take a glimpse at the Hudson Street
home in 1856.

Let us enter by the double door from the front
room into my Father's study.   We must close the
door and think.

He is not here at the moment : all is silent, yet the
room speaks of him in every corner of its solitude.
His strong individuality seems impressed on everything his hand might touch ; on the mighty Handel
on the mantel, in his majestic manliness, on the
volume of Bach on the pianoforte, on the keys
where his fingers play, as they unwind with love
and learning the intricacies of prelude and fugue.
And those books ! What voices, above all, have
they ! Large MS. volumes,[1] representing incredi-

[1] The MS. volumes alluded to are Dr. Hodges' own full Anthems,—many
of them being settings of whole Psalms, and several with orchestral accom-

ble labour of brain and hand.   They belong to the period we have read of, that seemingly wonderful life in the other sphere : a life wonderful, not so much for outward demonstration, as for erecting these monuments of inexhaustible musical power and fertility.

The accompanying poem of "The Cat's Fugue" is one of many—humorous and clever as they all were—thrown off by my Father, as he sat with his family around him, on those cozy "Evenings at Home," in his little gray house in Hudson Street, New York, near old St. John's Park.

With the bright lamp burning and casting a shaded light on the group around the table, and with the curtains drawn, how pleasant it all looked ! In the central place—and truly the central figure— was the Doctor ; his thoughtful and merry face bending over his paper, as his pen scratched away, taking down the rhymes which flowed so freely on. Every now and then, as if thinking a while to get the lines more smoothly written, out would come the gold snuff-box, and he "took a pinch" as only a gentleman can take it.

paniments ; Services ; arrangements from the works of J. S. Bach ; Graun's "Te Deum," adapted to the English version ; Boyce's "Cathedral Coll." : from the old Notation ; Purcell's "Ode" ; "Organ Fugues" ; "Stringed Quartetts" ; besides smaller compositions for the Church : these present the work of a life time.

Any little incident in his circle of friends or his family furnished him with a subject for his poems ; and the getting it into poetic or rhythmic form was a pleasant rest, after a day of fatiguing brain-work.

If interrupted by an evening visitor (which, however, was constantly the case), how quickly, to quote from himself, "with humour and grace," was the welcome given ! Then came the nice little bread-and-cheese supper, and the glass of ale ; and with them the interesting and intelligent conversation, the original thoughts and flashes of wit ; the keen comments on the topics of the day, or the droll anecdote ; and, better than all, many a helpful thought and scientific suggestion, or sound bit of musical learning or advice, so pleasantly thrown in ; all tending to make up a delightful and protracted evening, often till after eleven o'clock ; the charm of which those who participated in it can never forget.

The poem is founded on facts. Greenfield was the home of Dr. S. P. Tuckerman. He was the sportsman, and he shot the cat.

THE CAT'S FUGUE.

Scarlatti.

There once was a man (so the story doth go)
Who shot at a *pigeon*, and yet killed a *crow ;*
But I 've heard of a man, who, far better than that,
Once fired at a *rabbit*, and murdered a *cat.*

Poor puss had been frolicking out in the sun,
And was flatt'ring herself it was capital fun ;
When she came in the view of our sportsman's keen eye,
Who cried, " There goes a rabbit ! " and straightway *let
    fly.*

The people of Greenfield, amazed and perplexed,
All shook their wise heads to think what would come
    next ;
And the penitent marksman was heard to exclaim,
" Woe is me ! woe is me ! that I shot such queer game ! "

" Now, George ! Up and run for a surgeon, George, run !
And bid him to come, and see what 's to be done."
So George he did run, and the surgeon he came ;
But I can't for the life of me tell you his name.

He looked in the eyes and he opened the jaws,
And he felt for a pulse in the cold, clammy paws ;
And then, with deep feeling and pathos, he said,
" In my humble opinion this creature 's stone dead."

Now this puss was a fav'rite, a pet, and all that ;
Indeed, you may say an *exemplary cat ;*
And soon the sad tidings were borne to her master,
Of all this most bloody and fatal disaster.

9

Surely, none that beheld him his grief could despise,
As he stood by the corpse, with big tears in his eyes ;
And the sportsman's soft heart, overflowing with pity,
Regretted that ever he 'd come from the City.

At length, when his feelings found vent, he exclaimed,
" That 't was *I* who the gun at the animal aimed,
And thus shortened the days of the dear little brute,
I will not, one moment, attempt to dispute.

" But surely it was not my wish or intent
To harrow your soul with so dire an event,
That I *feel* for your loss you shall soon be assured,
And thus we may hope that your grief will be cured."

Now, just at this moment, *a five-dollar bill*
Was transferred to the mourner with hearty good-will.
The effect was electric, like magic, so strange,
From sorrow to gladness, so quick was the change.

His tears now all dry, the man laughingly said,
That, in view of the cash, it was well puss was dead ;
And he added that now he would sell off his *sheep*,
And a good breed of *cats* he would henceforward keep.

Then, addressing our sportsman, with humour and grace,
" I hope I shall *frequently* see your sweet face ;
For whenever you wish for some game that is nice,
I will find you a cat *at the very same price.*"

E. H.

May 22, 1856.

We have been favoured by a correspondent with
the annexed extract from the *Christian Alliance*

and Family Visitor. The letter is dated at Clifton, Bristol, and is given under the head of " English Correspondence" :

" It must be gratifying to our estimable friend, Dr.
Hodges, to find that notwithstanding his long absence
from his native land, he is still remembered by the in-
habitants of Bristol ; and it is also gratifying to his friends
here to find that they thus bear testimony to the worth
and excellence of their former townsman."

In speaking of Bristol Cathedral, the writer in
the *Alliance* says :

" The Cloisters have some fine old buildings, which recall the days of the Tudors. Here we saw the Prebendal
house (built on the Norman sub-structure of low arches
on which stood the Monk's Refectory) formerly occupied
by the learned and accomplished Dr. Hodges, now Organist of Trinity Church, New York. This gentleman is a
native of Bristol, and is, we find, held in affectionate remembrance by the best people of the City. I rarely, if
ever, have heard warmer encomiums pronounced by finer
spirits than I have listened to in reference to the Doctor."

A New York paper, about the same date, says :

" We met that sterling musician of the true ecclesiastical school, Dr. Edward Hodges, a few days ago, and are
gratified to find that he is still presenting a bold and
unflinching front towards the innovations of modern
improvements, as they are termed by some, in the
compositions for the Church. He considers himself 'a
sojourner' in this country, to use his own words ; and will
undoubtedly return to England ere long."

CHAPTER XI.

THE opening of the organs of St. John's Chapel in 1841, Trinity Church in 1846, and Trinity Chapel in 1855, were like milestones in my Father's musical life in New York. The former created great enthusiasm, as nothing approaching such organ-playing and effects had been heard in New York; and no doubt, as this was my Father's first large organ, he played with the freshness and genius of his, here, undeveloped powers, excited by the novelty of his position and the real grandeur of that noble instrument.

Regarding the Consecration Service of Trinity Church, the grandeur of which seems to have become traditional, I will only remark upon the rendering of the 95th Psalm, "Venite exultemus."

The music for this canticle chosen for the occasion was the double Grand Chant in C, by Jones, which my Father had arranged in eight parts. There were probably more than two singers on

each part, with his band of trained choristers behind (for the organ loft was quite full) ; and I can
truly say that the effect produced surpassed in
massive grandeur all that I have ever heard in the
way of chanting either before or since.   This was
not only produced by his splendidly-drilled choir
and the spirit that came from the magnificent organ,
but the majesty and meaning of the 95th Psalm,
placed as it is at the beginning of our service, was
powerfully brought out.   It must have been my
Father's spiritual conception and responsive devotion that sent King David's words home to our
hearts.   The organ was not finished then, but the
effects were none the less marvellous.   The moving
organ-part, perhaps from his coupling to the choir-
organ his triple-slat swell at octaves, formed a
mystic, rich background to the substantial body of
voices, just as rows of Doric columns are thrown
out into relief by an aerial sea of blue behind them.
Added to that, the rolling at intervals of the great
diapasons and the mysterious depth of the 32-ft.
pedals, like the sound of the distant sea,—all combined to create an ineffaceable impression upon the
mind, not only of devotional and musical grandeur,
but of my Father's interpretation of the service of
the Church, of which he was said to be a " true
liturgical minister."

Let me say a few words about the Consecration Service of Trinity Chapel. It is hardly known with what intelligent interest my Father entered into the work of the erection of this noble Chapel; so also he was a familiar figure about Trinity Church during the last years of the work there, watching with keen interest every department, and being consulted especially in the arrangement of the clock and bells. He took great pleasure in his friendship for Richard Upjohn, the eminent English architect of both buildings.

On Nov. 11, 1851, the Diary says:

"I went down to Upjohn's Office and inspected the plans of the new Chapel. Mr. Upjohn treated me very kindly and explained portions of them. I am to see him again. If I can only be trusted by this people, I think I can make a most delightful Organ effect there."

And when the Consecration Day came, with its unparalleled service of musical solemnity and beauty, yet remembered by many, organ effects were indeed produced which have never been excelled.

The occasion called forth the now published Anthem, Psalm 122, than which not one that my Father ever wrote seems more full of devotional science and lofty, chaste imagination.

From his original way of treating the subject, or

more properly from his own conception of the scene and Psalm, we seem to see the multitudes ascending to the Temple, and to hear their tramp and catch the sound of their voices as they sing their "Song of Degrees," "Let us go, let us go into the house of the Lord." My Father evidently saw the picture in his own mind, and the rendering of his music places it before us. All seem now to be gathered within the Temple walls. The masterly and manly solo of the Hierophant, "I was glad when they said unto me," echoing and expressing to the multitudes their own sentiments, is followed and accompanied by a chorus of priests and singers in true antiphon: "Our feet shall stand in thy gates, O Jerusalem." This is a scientific and well-worked fugue, purely diatonic, and most interesting and enticing to sing, the Hierophant leading to the close.

The service for Jerusalem proceeds, the Hierophant stating in a bold and original recitative the glories of the city: "The seat of Judgment— the throne of David." Three priests respond in an exquisite trio: "O pray for the peace of Jerusalem." Of course a little fugue comes in; but in this case it seems particularly to exemplify the meaning of the fugue in Divine worship; the voices echoing and following and answering each other; a

little triad in itself, a union of science, voice, and
spirit, as they blend together so softly at the last,

"O pray!—pray for peace!"

After this comes what is the crowning beauty of
the anthem—the Peace Chorus. This is virtually
the last movement, being interrupted by the lovely
little solo, "For my brethren and companions'
sake," which was composed for and sung by the
writer at that time. This is followed by the final
chorus for "Peace." The Composer supposes it
the prayer in heart of the vast multitude: "Peace
be within thy walls, and plenteousness within thy
palaces." It is a gem in sacred composition, it
embodies an ideal which can be comprehended by
few and only by those who are capable of forming
or perceiving a religious ideal. It is in the key of
C, and in $\frac{6}{4}$ time. There is a flowing, gently-moving,
passing on, of harmony and melody; there are
interior passages of sixths in vocal and instrumental parts, which seem to be floating down and
around; moving, yet ever at rest—satisfying, yet
causing us to crave for more. There is the regular, continued, soft beat of the deep pedal notes,
but from his own magic, mystic power at his organ,
which none could imitate or understand, there were
produced, just as he said, "some most delightful
effects." How simple his words! His marvellous

ST. MARY'S, REDCLIFFE, BRISTOL.

combinations, his exquisite swell, his octave couplers, all were obeying him ; but there was a spirit
breathing out of those serried ranks of pipes around
and about him which was not of earth.   His hands
—and who that had watched and noticed could
forget them ?— moved or, as he used to say,
" crawled," over the keys ; but his face, illuminated
as it was, showed above all where the spirit had
caught its inspiration ; and back of him, above and
around, the words, " Peace ! Peace !" seemed to be
wafted downwards as though on angel's wings,
suggested by the falling chords of sixths and those
marvellously beautiful organ effects, " Peace be
within thy walls."   But, as he said, " Peace is no
time of idleness, but of steady occupation," the
same pleasant little fugue comes back, inverted
this time, for to him it was as easy one way as
another, and, winding up with this happy employment, in almost unbroken silence the peace-laden
chords die away.

With a pathetic and prophetic spirit he gathered
around him on this occasion all his four children,
seeming to realize it would be perhaps his last
memorable service in the parish.

And it was so.

On the title-page of his own copy of this anthem,
my Father has written :

"The sermon reported to have occupied twenty-four minutes; the Anthem, twenty-two minutes. Balance in favour of the former, two minutes."

It was my Father's habit to go to the Vestry of old Trinity Church before morning service, to have a few pleasant words with the clergy.

I have watched him pass down the south aisle, carrying his broad brimmed hat sometimes on the head of his cane, and occasionally passing his hand through his hair—as he came from pillar to pillar, perhaps touched by the rays falling through the colored glass; and I, with others, have realized what a picture his form, face, and presence left on the mind, and how he harmonized with his surrounding of church architecture.

Arrived at the organ loft he seemed to belong to the organ. His large choir, including his boys, were in their proper places, and we all felt like soldiers on duty and stood to our guns. He was truly a beneficent "monarch of all he surveyed," and he met answering looks of devotion from all on whom his bright glances fell.

Looking at the paper containing the "Psalm and Hymn," I have heard him, with a quizzical expression, say:

"What shall I do with *that?* It is neither praise nor prayer!"

What a glorious thing it is for us all to look back upon that we sang with "*Dr. Hodges at Trinity Organ!*" That we were close to him as he manipulated the stops and played his inimitable "opening Voluntary." Have we ever *heard* one since? It was a poem—a prayer—and an artistic epilogue. Then the rendering of Ps. 95, who else ever gave it such a grand meaning? If it came to our lot to sing one of his own *Services*, what a pleasure it was; and though the playing of *King*, and *Rogers*, and *Gibbons* was superb and put new life into the old masters, still we preferred *his own*, and revelled in *them*. He was very loath to use his own Services; we had to beg for them. Then the "giving out" the tune! no one else even thought of such a thing! It is a lost art! but it was superb! Oh! the *sound* of that organ! will it ever entirely die out of our ears? No wonder that the people below wished over and over again that the choir would "stop singing, and Dr. Hodges play the hymns alone!" The concluding Voluntary was the summing up of all, for it seemed always as if the service had *inspired* it. Sometimes it was overpowering in its grandeur. It had the *genius through* it, the same kindling life, whether the music were Bach, or Handel, or his own. Those great minds again spoke in living voice ; or his own thoughts partook of the grandeur of theirs ; only having more freshness and freer modulation. No wonder people flocked to old Trinity, for, musicians or not, they knew they were in presence of a rare and great mind ; and for me, all I could do, was to go far away in the organ loft or down in the church and bury my face, and listen ; following, as well as I could, his overwhelming richness of improvization, or extempore, thorough fugue-power. Ah, those days ! Days, indeed, never to return.

He had a magnetic hold on his choir. It was a very different thing to any other " Church engagement." He took them as *human nature* as well as *singers.* There was one faithful bass whose voice was not acceptable, and whose pocket was low : and my Father gently silenced him and paid him on from his own pocket.

There was an old dog named " Bouncer " down at Trinity, and every Sunday morning my Father put a " cracker " in his pocket for Bouncer. Bouncer died at last, and the Sexton so grieved at his loss, that my Father gave him another dog. This was an intelligent dog, a real *church* dog. During service he lay in the porch ; and when service was over, he would guard the entrance under the organ, suffering no stranger to remain inside who did not remove his hat.

After I had some little organ experience I said to my Father, " Sir, I have beaten you at last ! "

" Very extraordinary ! " he said. " What have you done ? "

" I have played the people out, Sir."

(Something my Father never did.)

CHAPTER XII.

DR. HODGES AT ST. PAUL'S CHAPEL AND TRINITY CHURCH.

MY Father had great power at the organ in governing a large body of people singing. He said it was *an art*, but to him it seemed *nature*.

It was evinced grandly on one occasion, on which the writer was present, and one never to be forgotten, viz., the Convention held in St. Paul's Chapel, during which that scene took place which inaugurated the painful drama ending in the suspension of our esteemed Bishop of New York. The Church was crowded in every part and intense excitement prevailed; the Bishop on this occasion having maintained his position with a decision and manliness seldom witnessed. Giving no time for further remark, he said, in a full tone of voice, "Let the *Gloria in Excelsis* now be sung!"

Before my Father could get to the keys, or rap for wind, this hymn was begun by a voice below, and taken up by many others. I watched my Father as he first felt softly for the key in which they were singing, then by degrees he led them, till, backed by the organ, the voices all swelled in ; every one in the crowded body of the Church and in the crammed galleries above, joining in the sound. It was grand in the words " Heavenly King ! God, the Father Almighty," rich and subduedly grand in the prayer part, and culminated when my Father, catching the full significance of the scene and the power of the words, rolled out his full organ at the words, '' Thou only, O Christ, with the Holy Ghost, are Most High in the glory of God the Father." The effect was superb. The music of course was the " Old Gloria in Excelsis," known and sung by every one in the Church ; and the power or volume given to it by that unity was immensely enhanced by the deep feelings which were then stirred.

Here is an extract from his Diary, which emphasizes in satire one spirit of the times.

" *September 20, 1853.*

" I received by post two pamphlets by a Brooklyn Rector with a copy of the *Protestant Churchman*, containing an article commending the Pamphlets. These have given me some reading, but not much of either profit or amusement. One Pamphlet contains an essay *against* the Daily Service in Churches, and this by a clergyman !

" In the course of the evening, I finished the perusal of the two Pamphlets above mentioned. They are lamentable specimens of uncharitableness, and are directed against the High Church party. The animus may be gathered from the following supposititious prayer of such a man as the Author, gathered in a great degree from his own words :

" Prayer of an Evangelical Protestant Episcopal Pharisee :

" ' God ! I thank thee that I am not as other clergymen are ; formalists, ritualists, rubricists, semi-papists, or even as these Tractarians and Ecclesiologists : I keep no fasts, or Saints-days ; I cannot intone the prayers, and I would not if I could : I abhor and detest the Daily Service ; I believe in experimental religion and a change of heart ; and I give a portion of what I possess to Bible and Tract Societies, and the great Evangelical Institutions of the day.'

" It is a fair specimen of the spirit of the Pamphlets."

I cannot refrain from copying the following page from the Diary :

" September 22, 1853.

" Mr. Cook mentioned to me some touching circumstances connected with his family. He came from Norwich, has been here a little over three years, has gone to several churches (residing as he does on the Eastern side of the City, and a long way from Trinity,) but finally fixed himself at Trinity, because the music there affected him deeply—had been accustomed to take a little son of his about six years old with him, who likewise enjoyed the music excessively, and who would catch the melodies of the chaunts and shout them out at home, besides delighting to describe to his mother for hours together how beautiful the music was. The child died of croup, after a very brief illness ; and just before his death, begged to be carried to Trinity Church, that he might hear once more Dr. Hodges play, ' Praise the Lord, O my soul.'

'And now,' said the father, 'I go to Trinity and still enjoy the music, and can never express to you the pleasure it has afforded me ; and I often fancy that my little boy is *there too*,—I think I can see him beside me.'

" I bless God for this little incident. It is encouraging. The little fellow at home used to sit upon a high seat and drum with his fingers upon the table as though playing upon an instrument ; and bawl out 'Praise the LORD, O my soul.'

" Doubtless he sings it still, but not in such gross strains as ours.

" The pure and seraphic enjoyment of that little fellow (six years old at the time of his decease) is to me a source of greater and holier gratification than all the commendations I have ever received ! The boy's name was Alexander Cook, his death was almost sudden, as he was ailing but little more than an hour. Happy spirit ! He has got ahead of me now, but I trust to meet him in the heavenly choir—and perhaps then may have to learn of him !

" Before two I was at St. John's, scribbling on the blackboard for my boys ; and in due time they came, when I gave them not only a pretty severe musical practice, but also some very serious admonitions. I have some boys to deal with whose domestic education is by no means what it should be. It was past three o'clock when I closed the exercise."

The mention of St. John's, and the " blackboard," and the " practice " and the " admonitions " opens up a chapter in my Father's New York life which, incomplete as this sketch is, should not be passed over unnoticed.

The musical training he gave his Trinity boys

was valuable for all their lives ; but that seemed, when they afterwards spoke of him, almost ignored in the face of the great love they all cherished for him, and the veneration they had for his memory. A strict disciplinarian, whose laws were made to be enforced, he was yet their loving and sympathetic friend. How they love now to speak of the little treats and pleasures he gave them, especially his regular habit of taking them to have an ice-cream feast on his birthday, July 20th. Wherever or in whatever situation you meet an " old boy " of Trinity, whether in Orders or in business, there is but one story of their unfailing love for " the Doctor " ; of the words he said ; of his quaint bits of fun and repartee ; of his good advice ; of his sound admonition and good counsel for life ; and of the living example he set them by the justice, integrity and high principle of his own character, which all the time lay open before them. His trials and annoyances were many, but his greatest happiness out of it all must have been the consciousness that he was sowing good seed for future years. He had a real sympathy for the young ; and his ways, so singularly transparent, appealed to their boyish natures ; at the same time they dreaded his reproof and owned his severe judgments right. One way he had was of keeping all the money the bad boys paid in for fines, to buy prizes for the good ones.

Though now grown up and married, and plunged in the thick of the hard battle of life, I have found over and over again, that this one spot of love for my Father keeps green in their hearts. The Bible he gave—the writing he wrote—the likeness of him, treasured up—all say one and the same thing : that the memory of " the dear Doctor " and old Trinity will not fade away with years.

My Father's influence as a warm, living, and loving tie between our two countries, is a thought impressed deeply upon my mind.

By one writer he is called " an Exotic." And so he was. Yet he took root in America so firmly that he seems to be absolutely claimed here. Some friends could not think it at all right that this " Memoir," for instance, should begin in England ! " He is ours," they say, " he belongs to us." And a grand tribute indeed it is to both parties, that, gaining popularity here, he kept it, in spite of his Toryism and his most pronounced characteristics as an Englishman.

One great reason for this was his sweet geniality, the freshness of youth brought up into manhood, which instantly affiliated him with the young, as well as with all that was generous and genuine and honest in man, wherever found.

It was a living power he carried with him,—that unique characteristic that, let one be but accidentally in his presence for five minutes, something he would say, some remark he would make, or some thought he would give out, would linger in the memory for life.

The "international" tie thus begun, was felt in his music, which was part and parcel of his nature. How, without that living genius and freshness, could he, in the early years of his work (the decade between 1840 and 1850) have created a love for, and eventually an understanding of, the severe English school of Cathedral writers, King, Gibbons, Boyce, etc., etc., until this time quite unknown in New York ?

Soon pilgrimages, Cathedral pilgrimages, were made by the young and enthusiastic, as well as the mature and more thoughtful of his friends, and a love and appreciation for our Church music (especially for our cathedral services), was intensified. They heard of him who had quickened this love, at Windsor, at Bristol, at York, and in London:—and every grand C organ they listened to had a pipe voiced to his name. While the echoing sounds in the vaulted cathedral roof fell on their ear they could only say, "The noblest exponent of that noble school has been transplanted on the western shore. The calm, still air is *here*—the rich, quiet breathing-in of music through the centuries ; but the rushing wind is *there.* The steady light of ever-new composition is *here,* but the quivering flame and living gleam is *there.*"

Twenty years pass. The workman may be removed, but God carries on the work ; and the tie is over and over again strengthened by the influx of excellent English musicians who have entered into the newly-opened field ; and " the cry is still, they come." Yet *his* name, who threw open the field, is not forgotten. It is yet a *living* name. He seems yet present with those who, when young, heard his familiar voice and his pleasant joke ; who knew his face and form, and the merry twinkle of his eye. And the pilgrimages have gone on, if but of a faithful few, here and there ; some crossed the sea to clasp the hand of their venerated musician once more, while yet warm in the flesh, ere his spirit caught the words, " Come up hither."

Another twenty years have passed, and the same strong tie of sacred music in the Church has led other faithful hearts from the Western land to the city of his birth, its surroundings, and the scenes of his early life, as depicted in these pages. And more, the memory of him, though personally unknown to them, has beguiled some true hearts to seek, amidst the rich historic associations of the spot, that quiet village churchyard of St. Mary, Stanton Drew, and the Latin cross, beneath the willow tree.

Pilgrims' feet will, I trust, yet tread the sod of that peaceful "God's Acre." And mingled with the "Beati mortui" in their hearts, they may also hear, as though gently whispered by the breeze, the voice from afar, "Come up hither."

CHAPTER XIII.

MY FATHER'S MUSICAL WORK.

IT would not be right to withhold from even this incomplete and general sketch of my Father's life, some of his thoughts, views, and opinions on the Theory of Sound, of Thorough Bass, and Harmony.

'T is true, few may be able to follow him ; and he seems to me, as I read his writings in those far-off days of his youth, like one who enters a vast hall of silence, where even the echo of his own footfall is not heard. " Composers," as he says, " are not often theorists." At the very door of his mind there seemed to stand an array—a galaxy of intellectual lights, avenues of thought, waiting to be explored. That accounts for his oft-expressed weariness ; they oppressed him so much that I have often thought it was only the outlet of his grand sacred music and his almost unearthly rest in that, that saved his mind. He prayed for a " capacious intellect." It was given him. It was a well balanced and a clear one, and this renders his writing

on subjects we do not really understand delightful
to read.   We are content to follow and be led by
him.   Many learned men make a subject appear
difficult and confused to us ; not so my Father.
With him we see, and by his eye we read.   It is
just the difference between a profundity which is
impenetrable and muddy, and the clear dash of the
mountain stream.   Where it stops in the deep hol-
lows of the rocks, it is pellucid, and clear, and sky-
reflecting, and we are content to gaze into it, or to
follow it to the shore of profound thought, open, as
he says, to His eye, " Who knoweth all things."

I quote from the Diary so early as August, 1825.
My Father had been suffering from great depres-
sion of mind.   He had given a lesson in Thorough
Bass before breakfast, but after that he says :

" My day was good for nothing.   My usual flow of
spirits was gone, and I was altogether miserable."

He was one of those whom Keble describes as

" By nature strung too high,
By suffering brought too low."

His Diary continues :

" In the evening I walked out alone on the turnpike
road above Park St., and as I walked I meditated, and
became more tranquil.   Then I sought to apply my mind
to some useful topic, and adverted to the received principles and notation of

TEMPLE CHURCH, BRISTOL.

THOROUGH BASS.

"It has frequently occurred to me, that as at present taught and practised, the Science (if it can be so designated) is a confused mass of barbarous dogmas, its very first principles being as yet very unsettled. One writer contends *this* way and another *that*, which surely could no longer be the case, were the rules laid down, founded in nature and in truth.

"Rameau, in his dogma of the existence and stated progression of one grand fundamental bass, did much to check the progress of research and restrain the flight of genius.

"Still this was entirely independent of the figuring or notation, except in so far as it may have induced him to give to certain disputable combinations, certain determinate roots from which would follow certain resolutions (as in the case of the *added sixth*, which, though by the best masters made to *ascend*, yet, according to his theory, must, I apprehend, remain stationary). *De gustibus non disputandum est.* Music is unquestionably a matter of taste, but when a man has a system in his head, may not he make his taste bend to his theory?

"Methinks there is always great danger in systematising rapidly in the infancy of a science, and tho' the practice of Music has attained a wonderful degree of perfection, the science, even now, I consider to be but little farther advanced than its childhood.

"In suggesting therefore new principles, I would wish to do so with caution, and to consider nothing as established, but what is susceptible of some sort of proof.

"I have two things in contemplation relative to this subject: First, *A new Theory of Fundamental Basses*, and secondly, a *new Notation*.

"Rameau, in insisting dogmatically that every musical

chord has its fundamental bass, only went a little too far. If he had simply asserted that *many*, perhaps even most of them have, he would not have advanced anything objectionable, or which could not have been proved. But in striving to carry his favourite theory throughout, he had to combat with progressions which the nicest ear, and the strictest judgment, and the purest taste approve.

"The fact is, that laws in science are laid down as the result of experience. Our experience has enlarged, our laws are still contracted. Hence the outcry against the Schools, and the danger of utter insubordination to all classical authority. Even the 'mighty Masters' have, in the weakness of their great minds, occasionally descended to speak contemptuously of the laws of their Art, and feeling *themselves* above the region of the Schools, have falsely inferred that they were at liberty to pronounce them useless to everyone.

"But I am wandering. If I can elicit the principle upon which (unknown perhaps to their respective authors) the latest and best innovations upon the old practice have been founded, I shall go not a little way towards reducing to some order the confusion into which the science has been thrown, and perhaps adding yet more to the stock of materials out of which good music may hereafter be constructed.

"I say then, let it be supposed possible for a chord to have *two* real fundamental basses, or even more. It is but to refer to the well-known 7, 6^b, 4, 2, to be satisfied that it will easily explain what else is left enveloped in the mystery of creative genius. This supposed case will resolve all the old dogmas of *preparation* and *resolution*, seeing the teachers thereby implicitly laid down the rule, that no chord having two basses should be allowed, unless so much of them as belonged to the *previous bass* had been *previously heard.* So far good; but when the ears of the public had been sufficiently accustomed to these discords in a *prepared* state, the Masters dished them up *unprepared.*

" I am not prepared to say to what consequences infringement of established rule may lead, though I fear it tends to the destruction of sound composition, whether or not, it makes a new code necessary, and a dissertation to show how far the practice may be extended with safety. This code I apprehended must be founded on the admission of the principle that there are two fundamental basses. Then the explanation of the $\frac{5}{4}$, $\frac{9}{3}$, $\frac{7}{6}$, etc., will be easily intelligible, and much of the mystification of modern dogmatism will be annihilated.

" I will not enlarge further upon this branch of the subject at present, but proceed to the subject of *Notation* as far as Thorough Bass is concerned.

" Here we have intricacies enough. We have first a string of figures, and then their qualifications, of ♯s, ♭s, ♮s, all to be read at a glance, and as instantly played, all along bearing in mind the signature at the clef. This is enough to puzzle any brain, and although I have myself mastered the difficulties, I always feel for a young person just entering upon them.

" Now as all the received combinations, though many, are composed but of very few *elementary intervals*, I thought of substituting for the mass of figures with their attendants, certain arbitrary characters or signs, to each of which shall be attached the idea of some given interval. And as the chords are composed of these few intervals, the *signs* of the chords, or the Thorough Bass notation (which is after all, merely a musical short-hand) shall be in like manner compounded of these characters. So if a combination consist of a major third or perfect fifth (which is a minor third above the major before mentioned,) and a 7^b, which is still a minor third above the fifth) the sign or notation of the chord would be first that of a major third, then that of a minor third above it (making together a fifth), and still above that another minor third. Here the student would have before his eyes the whole composition of the chord displayed, be the key what it might.

"On my return home, I devised some characters, but as they were hastily sketched, I found some objections arise in *compounding* them. I shall however (*Deo volente*) return to this subject at some future time. I calculate that not more than six or eight characters are necessary."

"*Jan. 12, 1826.*

"7, as a Musical Prime.

"I was all day busily engaged in studying the relations of musical sounds as developed upon a Monochord, and graduating a scale upon that instrument to afford facilities for future investigation.

"The more I reflect upon the exclusion of the number 7 from musical primes, and the oftener I hear the effect of the employment of that number, the more thoroughly I am convinced of the injustice of that exclusion.

"I have consulted Dr. Smith and Malcolm, yet does not their statement of reasons convince me. The latter says the result is inharmonious. I contradict it. That it is *natural*, the French Horn, Trumpet and Monochord abundantly demonstrate.

"Engaged in these thoughts, I entered deeply into calculations, though as yet without any regular method.

"I look for some way of perfecting, or nearly perfecting, the scale by the help of this same unfortunate number; and I have great hopes of introducing it into practice by means of the Organ.

" Hague came in whilst I was engaged in this specula-
tion, and (as I should myself have done not very long ago)
contended that a *good ear* only was necessary to a good
musician, and that all such mysterious calculations were
good for nothing. But in the particular object of my
research this is not true. There is no singer who makes a
perfect flat seventh, and the reason seems to be the continual reference in the early stages of vocal tuition to the
fixed tones, notes or sounds of some instrument. There
is not one performer in a hundred who has ever even
heard the interval, except perhaps from a Trumpet or
French Horn by accident, and then he has been universally
taught to consider it as a note out of tune, ' a false note.'
Where the ears have been thus trained, little is to be
expected but determined opposition to innovation.

" If however I can succeed in forming a scale easy of
introduction upon keyed instruments, and employ this
forbidden ratio, I may steal a march upon their ears, and
convince their judgment through the medium of sense.

" I do not however anticipate the accomplishment of
so much without a world of pains and trouble.

" At a little before three I walked out, and, as yesterday, gained the summit of Brandon Hill, took a pinch of
snuff, and came down again. I afterwards went into the
cathedral and heard part of the Service, but my head was
literally all ' sixes and sevens.' If it goes on at this rate
I shall be in danger of becoming mathematical !

" All the evening I was occupied upon the same topic,
and it did not forsake me even in bed. I begin to be
even expert in compounding ratios, though I find I must
do it my own way.

" When I look into other writers upon the subject, they
seem to me very muddy : diffuse where they ought to be
explicit, and explicit, or rather unintelligible, where they
ought to be diffuse and explanatory. I hope to be able

to make these things plainer to those who shall come
after me.

" *Jan. 13th.*

" Immediately after breakfast Wilkins took his lesson.
I explained to him, after I had examined his exercise, the
leading doctrines of Harmonics, and demonstrated them
to him on the Monochord. This lesson seemed to produce a prodigious impression on his mind, which probably
never will be erased. He will certainly not rest till he
has a Monochord of his own. After his departure I continued my speculations and operations upon the Monochord, and before night completed graduated scales for
dividing a string into 2, 3, 4, 5, 6, 7, 8, 9, 10, 11, 12, 13, 14,
15, 16, 18, 20, and 21 parts or any multiple of either of them.

" In this I have adopted what is perhaps an original
method. To avoid the confusion of so many subdivisions
in one scale, I have made longitudinal partitions, and kept
2 and its multiples (or sub-multiples) in one line, 3 and its
attendants on a second, 5 and its disciples on a third, 7
and its outlawed companions in a fourth, and 11, and 13
in a still further detached position, yet so as to be all
under command for experimenting on a single string.

" In consequence of my directions we had fish for dinner, a regulation which is to be observed on succeeding
Fridays.

" To-day I thought of embodying my musical matters in
the shape of an appendix to Dr. Calcott's Musical Grammar.
That work as far as it goes is very good ; but it contains no
more than the orthography of the language, or at farthest,
the declensions of the nouns and conjugation of the verbs.
The syntax is wanting. This deficiency I think I may
supply. Calcott has not touched upon the Laws of Composition ; neither has he a syllable upon Harmonics.

Thus the two extremes of the system he has altogether avoided.

"I was all the evening at my Monochordial calculations till my head was fairly confused.

"*Jan. 14th.*

"Still it rivets my attention. De Boudry accompanied me to a book-seller's to look for some tables of Logarithms, to employ them in my musical calculations."

"*In my Study, Nov. 6, 1835.*

"Mrs. Butterworth and her daughters attended me at eleven o'clock, and had a further lecture upon Harmonics. They seem to comprehend the drift of my chapter (in the 'Tentamen'*) upon the 'Natural Derivation of Intervals' very well indeed. I fancy that I really have succeeded in making perfectly intelligible to ordinary capacities and ordinary *attention*, a subject hitherto treated so universally in an *abstruse* manner as to be, as it were, completely locked up from the great bulk of even musical people. This may encourage me to proceed with the work, which I have so long intermitted."

* To my great regret this valuable and much-needed work on Thorough Bass has not yet been found amongst my Father's effects.

CHAPTER XIV.

"In the beginning was the Word."

1829.

THIS Anthem conveys — as do all of my Father's—by even a cursory study, this direct impression : that before he put a pen stroke on paper, he had a clear and full conception of the whole subject in his mind, not only technically, as to the art of composition, but of the higher art of conception of an Idea. He had a wide mental field, and on it he erected his visual structure.

The Anthem is in the key of C, $\frac{3}{4}$ time. It opens *piano* and *crescendo* on the simple bass octave, the pedal bass C remaining steady for fourteen bars, including the introductory six bars by the organ. The upper part of this ascends chromatically with harmony, to the middle C. Here the voices all come in very softly, "In the beginning" in octave and unison, but follow up the course indicated to the next octave, arriving at the C to give emphasis to the words, " The Word was God" (*ff.*). These words once repeated in unison and octave, carry the treble to G, the accompaniment being bold and effective, while, the climax being reached, the impression left is as grand as it is satisfactory.

This development,—capable of any degree of fulness—though not resembling Haydn's " Fiat Lux " in the Creation, bears a striking likeness to it in conception. Haydn's is an immediate burst of Light. This has preparation. It has been foretold, and comes gradually. It certainly needs Orchestral accompaniment to bring out the effects, which lie hidden within it. It is easy to believe that, even here, my Father did not give full sway to his conception, although there is sufficient to indicate its nature, as far as he has revealed it ; and while reverently yielding to his favourite master, Haydn, and not improbably taking an idea from him, yet the leading thought was also *his own*, and no doubt carried him farther, and wider, and higher ; as *he* contemplated not the illumination of our universe alone, but the Eternal Heavenly Radiance of the " Light of the World."

The second movement (in ordinary tempo, in C, marked Gt. Diapasons), " And the Word was made Flesh," consists of an interesting, thorough

little Fugue in A Minor, exceedingly pleasant to
sing, and having an Obligato Bass accompaniment.
The Bass leads in the Fugue, which proceeds regularly, and the movement, ending on the dominant
major, introduces a still longer and more elaborate
and spirited Fugue, "We beheld His Glory," the
tempo a little faster.   The Alto leads.

Some striking effects are produced in this movement by the union of voices, rather *staccato*, "We
beheld," and by the introduction of solo passages,
which add beauty to it, as well as relief at the
words, "The Glory as of the only Begotten of the
Father."   These words carry a second subject,
which rather accompanies the first than is strictly
worked out itself.

It is only by the silent study of such a movement
as this in my Father's works that his intellectual
power can be known ; just as in playing or listening to the noble Fugues of Bach's "Wohltemper-
irte," the mind refuses, being unable, to follow the
beautiful working of the parts, filled as it is with
the dazzling harmony of the whole ; or, it may be
that the unity, power, and beauty of the whole,
render it impossible to divide the mind into a true
perceptiveness of the several parts.

This movement is virtually the conclusion of
the Anthem ; the two subjects now work faith-

fully together ; the spirited flow of them only once broken by a unity of vocalization on a *fortissimo* passage. The conscientiousness of this Fugue work is somewhat marvellous, both as a study and an example, the accompaniment following rigidly the vocal parts. A working through them is at last gained, by a hold of four bars on the dominant bass, and the end is reached at a *grand fortissimo*, where unity is given to the whole by the free accompaniments being the same as stood by " The Word was God " at the beginning, and now giving grandeur and finish to the end at the words, " Full of grace and truth."

But there follows, what is the *middle* part ; a slow quartette in C Minor, unaccompanied, " For the law was given to Moses," followed by the words, " But grace and truth came by Jesus Christ." The smooth and graceful phrase which expresses these words is remarkable for this, that it really seems to *enforce* a reverent expression and bow of the head at the pronunciation of the Holy Name. It speaks alike for the reverential tone of my Father's mind, and for the due attention he gave to words and accent, that attention, in some later writers for the Church, being much neglected, or made subservient to the flow of musical ideas, not always appropriate to them.

I hardly know whether this beautiful movement would be called a Fugue or Imitation ; at any rate, the one pervading phrase is taken by all parts, sometimes three at once, sometimes inverted, and displaying what Samuel Wesley called "great ingenuity"; but the words would be worthless and have no meaning, unless the *thought*, bearing the intellectual and artistic work *in itself*, expressed a loftier sentiment. The second Fugue "And we behold His glory" is returned to, and the Anthem is finished.

Of a beautiful Anthem composed in 1851 my Father writes :

"*Dec. 5.*

"I at length made a beginning of the Composition of an Anthem (from Ps. cxxxiv) for the Consecration of the Assistant Bishop of New York. Poor stuff!"

The anthem was, however, not used until the opening service of the General Convention, which was held in Trinity Church, October 5, 1853. This was one of the "grand services" of old Trinity. I quote from one of the papers of the day :

"There could not have been many short of 3000 persons present. In the procession of Bishops nearly every State was represented, Bishop Boone of China, the ex-Bishop of Madras, the Rev. Dr. Spencer, with Bishop Brownell, taking the ante-Communion Service. The Ven. Archdeacon of Middlesex, Dr. Sinclair, read the Litany ;

after which the 100th Psalm ('With one consent') was sung.

" At this time the Chancel presented a very imposing appearance, the sunlight streamed through the stained windows in its south side, and rays of blended gold, crimson, purple and ruby, fell in haloes around the heads and forms of the Bishops, many of whom presented an exceedingly venerable appearance. It was a scene worthy the inspired pencil of a Raphael or a Titian.

" The music was uncommonly fine ; Dr. Hodges, of course, presided at the Organ, and he had about him a choir of over thirty singers. The Te Deum and Jubilate were Nares in C, and were given with great force and effect. The Old Hundreth filled the whole church with such a truly congregational volume of vocal praise as has rarely been surpassed. The Anthem by Dr. Hodges himself was a beautiful composition. The call to ' Praise the Lord,' starting with a single male voice, went on increasing in number and power until the full chorus burst forth, ' Lift up your hands in the Sanctuary and Praise the Lord.' The final ' Hallelujah, Amen ' was the crowning beauty."

Speaking of his composition, he says in his Diary :

" Feb. 25, 1853.

" My slowness of composition is most lamentable. So I presume it will be always, unless I can secure more consecutive time for study, and greater privacy than I now enjoy when engaged in composition.

" How often do I think with regret of my beautiful old Study in the Cloister at Bristol, with its delightful seclusion ! "

Yes ; there was a vast difference between the old "Study in the Cloisters" and his small one in his New York home. It is noticeable that all my Father's elaborate works or compositions, consisting of full Anthems, of whole Psalms, and all those composed for events in the Royal Family, date from the Cloisters. No wonder that he recalled "its delightful seclusion."

From his deep bay window he saw nothing but the trees and broad walks of the Bishop's garden ; at the other end—for the room extended the whole depth of the house—were the Cloisters, and the rarely-broken quiet of the Cathedral close.

In this study, he formed a picture himself. I can see him now in my mind's eye as he stood at his high desk, writing, clothed in his long, black velvet study gown, his unique, and, to me, always beautiful and intellectual head bent forward as he wrote. How soft and wavy his hair rose from his temples ! No matter how the aspect of that Musæum-like room affected you, with its wall-lining of book-shelves, its bits of classic sculpture, its musical curiosities, its piano-forte (standing bravely out in the centre ; on it, Horn's Edition of *Bach*) and its other attractions of study or comfort, you would pass them all by, and your attention would be fixed on that standing, reverent figure at the desk.

PRIORY LODGE, BRISTOL.

I always knew when my Father was engaged on a musical work. There was an abstraction about even his manner; I had an innate feeling that I must not disturb him. His desire for solitude was as marked then, as was his love for social pleasure at other times when his mind was free.

When composing, it was never possible to get any idea of his work, he touched the piano so seldom. As a child I was impressed with the marvellous grandeur of the final rendering, when the whole work seemed to have been perfected in that magic silence and seclusion. This struck me forcibly in his noble translation of the 136th Psalm; I marvelled how in the unbroken quiet, day after day, night after night, a labour of such power and magnitude could have been brought into existence. I might have heard little suggestions of it, a scrap of fugue, or a *thought*, unknowing that it was a thought; but of its entirety I had no notion until it burst upon me as a whole, in its grand verse and antiphon.

The Anthem, " For His mercy endureth for ever," which was composed at Bristol, is a prince among my Father's anthems; and I remember listening to his large band of amateur singers and friends, and being arrested by his original way of disposing of " Sehon, King of the Amorites, and

Og, the King of Bashan," which he put to the Grand Chant by Humphrey, while the fine antiphon in the chorus was not interrupted in its course.

I do not wonder my Father recalled his old study with regret.

His power over people was very marked. Nervously quick and full of musical irritability, he was patience itself, and nothing but kindness and goodness could come from his heart. But it was not so much the latter characteristics as his power, his knowledge, his precision, his own highly gifted natural self that won the field, and made all who approached him, willing and whole-hearted admirers. How his brilliant eyes would flash! and though always clear in explaining a difficult passage, how impetuously and imperiously he would dash through intricacies intelligibly and unfalteringly, as though saying "This has to be *done*, whether you will or no," and *through* it would go. They saw the Master in him, in the flash of his eye; heard it in the ring of his voice, and felt it in the swift and unerring mastery of his Fugues, from the announcement of the text or "subject," until the exhaustive and magnificent close.

I find in his Diaries very much that would be of interest to composers; little items connected with

Fugue subjects; notes of times when it is easiest to write, etc. For himself he decides that *midnight* is the best time when, from the surrounding silence and his own solitude, he finds his ideas flow more easily.

It was in his New York home that on one particular occasion I heard and saved that succession of chords to which I gave the name of " My Father's Midnight Chant."

The evening was over; stray guests had departed, having enjoyed the " chat " and the bread-and-cheese and ale supper; the usual hour for Evening Prayer had come, and gone, and the last foot-fall had been heard on the stairs.

Then my Father retired to his study, as was his wont, for he always much enjoyed reading alone. I also had gone to my own room above his study, and after a time, had put out my light.

From a half-asleep state, I was brought to consciousness by an indistinct sound of rich and beautiful harmonies, which seemed to suggest a picture of a still lake over which organ-chords were floating from some half-hidden monastery chapel. I at last realised the truth. " It is my Father's midnight music ! "

I quickly jumped up, struck a light, and ere he had gone from the fascinating chords, I had them written down. I am sure the modulations must have given him pleasure, or he never would have repeated them often enough for me to write them. They *are* very grand ; and he seemed to have more than two handfuls of splendidly-distributed harmony. I had them safe before my eyes ; and when he had finished his—to me—unrivalled and unsurpassable excursions into fields of unworldly sound, he sang, as usual, his "Nunc Dimittis," came softly up stairs and passed my door. Then he quietly closed his own, and I heard the click of his little bolt.

Then I thought myself to sleep on the question as to what it was that gave so unique and unsurpassable a grandeur and beauty to my Father's *improvisations*. That word, however, is not the right one. They were more properly *meditations*. They represented trains of thought, moods of the mind, grades of deep religious emotion, powers of the intellect and aspirations of the spirit, and even seemed to express the relation of the soul to the Great Arbiter of our destinies in some state of being beyond this earth.

There was something *living* and *speaking* through his chords and modulations and consecutive, thoughtful meditations which could never be conveyed by another. Melodies would gleam out here and there, speak to each other, and die away in the environing clouds of soft, varied harmony—like sunset hues—all distinct, and blended by his perfect finger-power and graduated touch, while suspicions and intimations of all the resources of musical art, the developments of science, a height of imagination, a depth of feeling, a width of sympathy, were all condensed, as it were, into one hour's expression in the night time; a time when the soul withdraws to its *solitude*, so truly called "The Antechamber of the Deity," when "none but God is near."

And it was this exquisite "finger-power" that seemed to probe the depths of harmony ; to search them, and exhaust them, bringing to the surface its reasons and its meaning in a way and with a power that, to my mind, no other hand has ever possessed.

He said to me once, "the grandest music has never been written." So he taught me to realize what I had already seen in him : *the consecrated gift*, and its ultimate destiny and development.

In the morning, before my Father had come down, I put the MS. on his desk. He sat down and, looking at it, said, "What's this?" He played it, and continued, "It is *bad!* These are perfect fifths!"

Evidently he had no remembrance of it at all :

while I, having written it under the fear that he would stop playing, or roam yet farther away, when I should lose it altogether, had to get it down as quickly as I could, the modulations being so close and unexpected. The *fifths* had come from this cause, and, of course, were mine. I knew the chords were rich and substantial, and they were *his own :* and I am thankful I rescued them.

When he was composing the Anthem "*I was glad*" (Ps. cxxii) for the consecration of Trinity Chapel, I noticed how rarely, and especially how softly, he touched his piano-forte : just a *thought* or a suggestion of a phrase would come now and then ; and what a treat it was when he would play a movement entire !

A remark, made only lately by one of his warm appreciators, is singularly true :

"Your Father wrote for Scholars."

Very truly, my Father wrote "for Scholars," so far as intellectual acquirements of a high grade are perceptible in his music. He believed and taught, that the *intellect* should be used in the Praise of God as much as the emotions and aspirations of the soul and spirit. He believed it to be, perhaps, God's greatest gift, to be consecrated to Divine Worship in every avenue of its development and thought. My great, Catholic-minded, worshipful Father! While he could soar to the highest, he could stoop to the lowest: and the chief reason why we do not hear more of his published music is, that people have not soul enough to throw into it its vital spirit of devotion. The great Bow of prismatic Light and Sound spanning the archway between the heavenly choirs above and our poor, imperfect attempts here, is one of many more colours than the Rainbow! My Father seemed to dream of it, and his writings give but slight intimations of the soaring thought of which his consecrated intellect was capable.

He *did* truly write "for Scholars"; but in the great field *outlying* the range of intellectual musical acquirement, he reigned also supreme. Instance that beautiful and touching incident of the little dying boy, "Take me to Trinity Church, that I may once more hear Dr. Hodges play 'Praise the Lord, O my soul!'" and remember how he said, "This little incident has given me more pleasure than any commendation I have ever received." What spirit is manifested by that simple confession, but that the great aim of all his acquirements was reached? He had drawn one soul nearer its Maker. It was the soul of a *little child*, and he did not despise one of those "little ones."

And how many more had he moved, all unknown
to himself, as his spirit, subtle as the wind, floated
through the Church, bearing aloft the incense of
"prayer or praise," just as the same wind, which
the Blessed Saviour, in that profound midnight
converse with the Hebrew Rabbi, Himself likened
to the Spirit, bears away on its breath the odours
of myriads of flowers in its onward, unseen path.

CHAPTER XV.

MUSICAL LIFE IN NEW YORK.

IN that alanthus-shaded street where the katy-dids and tree-toads chatted and argued until the day-dawn, lived the strict and scholastic Doctor, beloved and admired by all, in his unrelenting English dignity and geniality.

Yes ; and as the street was made lively from four in the morning by the fruit-seller's insistent cries, he would rise in the comparatively early coolness of those New York August days, and play his Fugue.

It was on the 23d that he was thus early at the keys, probably *minus* coat, and the Fugue of course was No. 23, in the key of B, Book 1.

Not yet aroused from my heavy forgetfulness, untraceable musical thoughts and suggestions seemed to be mixed up with my dreams. I did not know *what* I heard, nor where I was, as those streams of winding melodies and harmoniously flowing modulations passed through my mind   At last the truth fell in like a ray of light and I realized all, and said, " It is my Father; my Father playing his Fugue !"   And I listened in a state of restful and intellectual delight.   The reality was lovelier far than the dream, and the sound of my Father's fingers, so soft and masterly, will never pass from my memory, though they spoke so long ago.

And of all the Fugues so dear to me, there is none more dear than 23, in that soothing, lovely key of B, as it spoke to me on that morning.

There is a motion and a freshness in the air from the western window ; a glint of sunshine from the upper blue strikes through the half-closed blind, as the green of the vine is revealed on the trellis outside.   A sun ray falls athwart his desk, and, lying on the blotting sheet there, the eye catches sight of a *small home-made book.*

It lies before me now, though nearly forty years have passed since the musician's artistic fingers constructed it.

It consists of two pieces of cardboard neatly bound with a piece of broad twilled tape, and leaves very neatly sewed in with fine string ; just such an artistic, quaint affair, as only genius would devise, since it would despise a shop-bought article.

On the outside cover are the words :

" M. W. Topics.

Aug. 1856."

and inside is written

" Topics for possible Articles

in the

Musical World.

E. H., Aug. 21, 1856.

1. Plain Song . . . . . . Mch. 1857.
2. Gregorian Tones . . . . . Feb. 1857.
3. Numbers and Definite Proportions . 2, 3, 4, &c.
4. Music in Common Schools . . . (1)
5. Organ building.
6. Standard Organ . . . . . Sep. 1857.
7. Encouragement of Native Talent.
8. Psalm Tunes in C, in $\frac{3}{2}$ and $\frac{3}{4}$ compared.
9. Individuality in performance . . Jan. 1857.
10. Grammar of Music.
    Declensions, Government of cases, &c.
                                Touched Oct. 1857.
11. Skill in playing, not tested by *velocity* merely,
12. The teaching faculty . . . . June 1857.
            Self-taught artists and teachers.
13. Sol-Fa system.
14. Practical Thorough-Bass.
15. Theoretical Do. . . . . . (3 touched)

16. Musical Stenography.
17. Boston Music Hall and Organ.
18. Music Committees   .   .   .   June 1857.
19. Choir Leaders.
20. (See 17.)
21. Music Halls in general.
22. Ratio of expense decreases with increase of magnitude.
23. Vibrations, Pulsations, Undulations, &c.
    Matter of Sound .   .   .   Touched 4. 5.
                          And again.
24. Sir Isaac Newton and Prismatic Music.
25. Music of Moschetoes !
26. Calliope and Steam Music.
27. Polarized Light, and analogy with sounds.
28. Elocution and Singing.
    Touched by R. S. W. in his ' Spoken Music.'
29. Organ-grinding nuisance.
30. Crotchets and Quavers.
31. Tones and Semi-tones.
32. Sesquialtera, and other Organ names.
    Mutation Stops .   .   .   .   .   Sep. 1857.
33. Clerical interferences not always beneficial.
34. Can *every body* learn to sing ?
35. Clefs.   (The C Clef.)
36. Isle of Serpents !
37. Salable Compositions.
    Fashion in Church-world.
38. Audible limits of Scale. Birds. Crickets.
39. Old Hydraulic Organ.
40. Music of Fishes.
41. Definition of Music difficult.
42. Testimonials to men and things given too readily.
43. Different Systems adapted by various Music Teachers in public Schools.

93.   Organ Style of playing.
94.   Genius vs. Manufacture.
95.   Instrumentation and Orchestration.
96.   Choral Service.
97.   Modulation.
98.   Querstand.
99.   Editorship of Collections, Psalmody, &c.
100.   Orchestra   .   .   In part only.   1857.
101.   Organs as Church *Furniture*,
            as Church Instruments,
            as Orchestral   "
            as Domestic   "
102.   Concerts ; Management, Programmes, Expenses.
103.   Notation.   Complex.   .   .   .   Nov. 1857.
104.   Whistling !!!
105.   Out of Tune.
106.   Prize Compositions.   . May, 1858."

Subjects not before Mentioned.

"1.   Harmonics.
2.   Singing and Sand.
3.   Study and Practice.
4.   Progress of Music in the Church.   Review of G. F.
        Bristow.
5.   Sympathy.
6.   Pianology.
7.   Suspensions.
8.   Motives for Studying Music.
9.   The New and the Old.
10.   The Old and the New.
11.   City Hall Bell.
12.   Choral Service.
13.   Anglican Chaunt.

14. Music and Morality.
15. Plagal Cadence.
16. Keynote.
17. Ancient Choirs.
18. Modern Choirs.
19. Clerical Management of Music.
20. Choir Places.
21. Drums.
22. Teeth.
23. Taste.
24. Musical Legislation.
25. Oratorios.
26. Music Committees.
27. How to hear Music.
28. Execution and Expression.
29. Clefs or Cliffs.
30. Plain Singing and Plain Song.
31. English Cathedrals.
32. Dr. Tuckerman's Lecture.   .   .   Dr. Guilmette.
33. Church Organs. Ordinary Church Organ.
34. Glance at Musical Grammar.
35. A Parable.
36. The Mouse and the Deacon.
37. Art Encouragement.
38. How to shorten Divine Service.
         (All published in the *Musical World*.)"

In the *little book*, I find the following Auto-
graph, which may be of interest to those who
cherish the memory of the musical clergyman, as
well as of his beloved friend the clerical organist.

BRISTOL CATHEDRAL.

"Suggestions for the Pen of ' H.' in the
Musical World.

1.   Difference between musical sentiment and devotional
feeling.

2.   Comparison of the advantages and disadvantages of
singing Chorales in Unison or in Harmony.

3.   Wherein exists the peculiarity of Cathedral Music.

4.   The little which English Cathedrals have done for
Cathedral Music.

5.   Desirableness of clerical skill in Music.

6.   Departed clerical composers and clerical organists.

7.   The superiority of Händel in the Majesty, and
Beauty, and Independence of Accompaniment.

8.   Charles and Sam. Wesley as Extempore Organists,
with Hints on Extempore Organ-playing.

Received from good Mr. Havergal, July 2, 1857, in a
letter, dated Worcester, June, 1857."

My Father had a very happy and original way
of calling us, *musically*, easily adapting our names
to a phrase in melody corresponding to them in its
syllables and accent.   This was curiously and effectively tried in St. John's Chapel, New York, one
Sunday morning during my Father's occupancy of

the organ-stool there, prior to the Consecration of Trinity Church.

My brother had taken his usual seat in President Moore's pew in the middle aisle, and I was with my Father in the organ gallery.   It was now the usual time for him to play the first voluntary ; and calling my attention, he said to me " I am going to call Jubal.   Watch him."   His voluntary proceeded as thoughtfully and smoothly as usual ; in the course of it the phrase,

which was his call for my brother, was repeated twice.   It was distinct, and at the same time so much a part of his improvization, that a general listener would not have noticed it at all.   At the first time my brother seemed arrested by it ; at the second he turned and looked up, but saw no sign.   When the call came the third time he deliberately took up his hat, and, leaving the pew, walked straight up to his Father and said, " Do you want me, Sir ? "   " Yes," said my Father, " Go home and get my gold snuff-box."   The errand was speedily executed, the house being so near St. John's Park.   He handed the snuff-box to his Father and returned to his seat.

The following is a copy of his note-sheet, which gives an idea of what he found or rather what he did *not* find in New York ; of his plan of attack, and his mode of reconstruction, remembering he alludes only to the " Music " of our Church :

" MUSIC—AS IT IS IN THE UNITED STATES.

Hindrances.

Absence of permanent Choirs.
   "   " endowed *Professorships*.
   "   " musical *Rubrics*.
' Anthem.'
   "   " authoritative standard.
False position of *choirs*.
Clerical ignorance !
Puritanical psalmody *first* on the ground.
Low standard of Organists.
Operatic importations.
Influx of Germans, etc.
Would-be *independence*.
Defective style of chaunting.
Pseudo *Gregorian* Music,
English *Cathedral School* neglected.
Two or three Services printed only.
Good books not to be had, except from abroad, and then half useless.
Strange notions afloat as to the propriety of *paying* musical officers of the Church,
Thorough training of *Boys* neglected.
Rarity of well directed efforts.
Holy Cross, Troy.
Holy Communion, New York.

Confusion of ideas concerning Anthems and Services.
        (An Anthem *read*.   Churchman.)
A whole generation necessary to work a radical change
for the better.

Remedies.

Found Professorships, especially in the Theological
        Seminaries.
Found Church *Schools*, having particular reference to
        Church Music.
Restore rubrics, and the Pointing of the Psalter.
Disengage Organists, etc., from necessary contact with
        secular music *for a living*.
Consider Music no longer as a mere stop-gap in Divine
        Service.

Adherents of exclusive congregational singing.
Musical reputation built upon false pretences.
Decay of English Cathedral Foundations. Possible fur-
        ther effect of California !
Cornwall's ' Warwick,' etc.   Power of early associa-
        tion.
Organ pitch raised ; and *why ?*
Projects of *New Notation*. (Zundel and von Heerin-
        gen, etc.).
Good Friday music."

I find in the Diary the following entry :

" February 1, 1835.

" I composed a Chaunt at Faustina's request."

My Father mentions no key, in connection with
this " request " for a Chaunt.   Therefore I cannot

identify his writing me one at this time with the one I refer to in my " Notes " in the pamphlet entitled,

"Kyries, Chaunts and Tunes by Edward Hodges, Mus. D." (Novello, Ewer & Co.).

It is quite possible I asked for "a Chaunt" at this time, although I have forgotten it ; the other parts of it all, I remember well ; so I copy my own words, and append the Chaunt in the much more beautiful original key ; one easily reached by English men and boys.

"One day, when we were living in the Cloisters, I heard my Father improvising on his Broadwood in the key of A♭. This key having a strange fascination for me, I quickly went up to his study door and knocked. He said 'Come in,' and I went in, and stood by him silently. He continued to play on for some little time ; and coming to a cadence, I thought he had finished, and said, ' I 'm so fond of A♭'; without speaking, he played on until his thoughts took a definite shape. Leaving the piano he went to his high desk, at which he always stood to write, and in a minute or two brought me this beautiful Chant. He had headed it 'Faustina's Chaunt. I 'm so fond of A♭.'

" Well do I remember his courteous and gracious manner as he presented it to me, which could not

have been more marked had he been addressing a
superior in age, instead of his own child.

"Years passed by.   He had gone to New York ;
the Chant had passed from his memory, but I had
kept it, and one day I placed it on the desk of his
Piano.   He played it, liked it, lowered the key to
G♭, and put it in his ' Trinity Collection.'   It soon
became a favorite, was copied into many collections,
and has been one of the most generally used Chants
in the United States."

From the *Musical Magazine* and *Quarterly Review*, 1826, I make the following extracts :

"Dr. Hodges's Opus. 1.

"Morning and Evening Service in C.

"With Two Anthems.

"It is refreshing to turn to the chastened Melody, fine
Counterpoint and proper clefs.   This is music to retire to
from dramatic noise and nonsense. Dr. Hodges, in a
short preface, very properly waives all apology for the use
of the legitimate clefs.   He opens his Te Deum with
plain, appropriate and effective harmony ; a solemn strain
of plain, full counterpoint. The fugal points, here and

throughout, are designedly brief, the lights and shades of Harmony judiciously contrasted, and the modulation sufficient and effective. The Te Deum is we think the best part of the Service ; and some of the musical phrases are of a very elevated character. It contains also a fine instance of Canon.

" The whole setting of the Psalm 'O give thanks,' to go no further, is a sufficient proof of the Composer's ability in the style to which he aspires. In the two Anthems the Doctor evidently rises in conception and grandeur. The melodies and harmonies in the opening chorus 'O give thanks' are both sweet and dignified. The close, in which due attention is given to the words, is grand. The Chorus, which concludes the Anthem, opens à-la-Händel too obviously. It is a dignified chorus in which the passage of Octaves forms a striking and grand contrast to the full Harmonies ; and the fugal point, though very simple, is on that account very impressive.

" The ' St. James Anthem ' opens with a short Overture, where again we are reminded of Händel as well as Corelli, and any attempt at originality is waived in favour of classic propriety. A fine chorus in C minor follows the Overture, and is sufficiently diverse in style from the preceding choruses. This is followed by a descriptive Quartette and Chorus in the major relative, in which the words ' Praise the Lord upon the Harp ' occur, and are of course adapted to imitative music, and with interesting effect. A fine double Fugue terminates the work. The Fugue is scientifically and effectively constructed throughout various modulations, and ultimately blends with the solemn Hallelujah, both vocally and instrumentally, and terminates with grandeur.

" Finally, if these compositions are not remarkably distinguished by originality, the apology is obviously that they are modelled on a style where originality can scarcely be expected. The severity of that style, introduced, or at least established by the Reformation, has banished quirks and fantasies in Ecclesiastical Music, and originality in the path of creative talent requires the most discreet management, even from the sublimest genius."

I have spoken of my Father's invention and use of little musical phrases to serve as *calls* for us. My own was the following :

His usual attention to the number 3 is apparent. The *third* time, my name came out with *great* decision !

I give the bare harmony.   Of course he filled it in as he list.

His call for my good second Mother was the leading phrase of his " Service in F."

My brother Jubal drew a most intelligent comparison between his Father and S. Sebastian Wesley, as musicians, the genius of Wesley, transcendant as it was, making him hold in even higher reverence and estimation the abilities and powers of his Father.   He saw where his Father's thorough fugue power came in, conveying the idea that he

BRISTOL CATHEDRAL.

had trained his intellect somewhat at the expense
of his imagination. He also recognized his Father's
greater profundity and grandeur, combined with
equal scientific skill : above all, he felt in his Father's
playing a soul-compelling power, which seemed
permeated with a spirit of adoring worship and
spiritual exultation. " Could the two be shaken
together, and their distinctive genius blended," he
said, " what two magnificent, almost superhuman
minds should we have ! "

My Father's voice as I remember it, was of a
high Tenor quality, exceedingly sweet, delicate
and plaintive in tone, and exquisite in Chromatic
passages.

In his Bristol Diary I often find :

" At the Cathedral this morning I took a stall
and sang Bass through the service." Showing its
compass, he constantly speaks of his taking Tenor,
Counter-tenor or Bass in his Anthem or Service
music, where a part was required.

A musical friend in New York once startled me
by saying " What an exquisite singer your Father
is ! " Until then I had not fully realized the veiled
and rarely-heard perfection of his voice.

As I have written much music and have not preserved any " reviews " or " critiques " but the

following, I am tempted to insert it here. I value it not only for its source, but because the writer, whom I have never discovered or known, seems to have read my mind, and interpreted my meaning.

My brother, the beloved Jubal, on leaving me one day, said, "Write ' Blessed are the pure in heart' *for me.*" In due time the music was written. It was first published by G. Schirmer, New York, and afterwards by my faithful old friend Dimoline, of Bristol, who sent a copy to Novello. It is for three voices. The notice which I copy is from the *London Musical Times* of Feb. 1, 1874. The words were written four years after my brother had entered that life which his "pure heart" on earth anticipated.

" Blessed are the pure in heart."

" Here is a truly charming little Trio. Its chief melody is most graceful, its harmony is fresh and decidedly modern in character, without being more chromatic than is necessitated by the phraseology of the top part, nor than is easy to sing and delightful to hear, and the effect of the combined voices is admirable.

" The merit of the music stands high, claims attention, and should secure wide acceptance for the piece. We feel the naturally devout expression of every phrase, though this is rendered in unconventional forms, and we are glad to find a writer who is so independent of custom's trammels, that she can set scriptural words to notes that flow from her heart, and so present them with an air of conviction in their truth."

13

CHAPTER XVI.

THE details of these very numerous inventions may to some seem tedious and unnecessary ; while to others they may be the most important part of all. Unless they are both clearly and wholly given, what is the use of noticing the inven-ventions at all ? We should thus leave one part, and a very important part of my Father's life out of sight altogether. It is very true, that the Mow-ing Machine, and the Screw Propeller, and the Dumb Waiter, and Sections in Ships, and the Roller Skate, and the application of Electricity, and the bleaching of India Rubber, and Iron Steeples and Stairs, and I believe dozens of others, all have respectively been done or brought into use years after he first recorded them ; but they are none the less *his ;* they occurred to *his* mind, and each one of these had *in* his mind its full de-tail and way of working, and received as much careful thought in kind, though not in degree, as his most carefully worked-out Fugue. Not to give the details then would be injustice to him.

The most remarkable points in it all, are: First, the fact that one who is known chiefly as an eminent Church Musician and Theorist should have thought out all those other things; secondly, his extreme youth; and thirdly, the state of knowledge then, and his solitude in Bristol.

It was not so remarkable that he should have soared into the regions of Acoustics, where Newton reigned supreme, or that the metaphysical part of music so fascinated him. We cannot see things as they were then, and as he saw them. We are in the light of the knowledge he foresaw, and in a very great degree enjoyed. His eye was prophetic, as his aims were unerring; and the result was sure, though the latter may have been gained by other ways than his.

Here is a little picture of his boyhood.

He is a lad of sixteen, and we see him making his way one night up to the roof of the old Bridge Street house, carrying something very carefully. Immersed in acids (according to his knowledge of Chemistry,) is a specimen of black, unsightly Caoutchouc.

Now he has determined in himself that this black stuff can be made *white*. It never has been done, but he has laboured for many months at it, and will not give it up.

He also writes his belief that it is capable of many different uses ; that it can take colours and be moulded into many shapes.   Up to the roof he goes early next morning and finds that this, one of his latest experiments, is partially successful.

Was not his forecast of India Rubber absolutely verified ?

The year 1821 was for Dr. Hodges as an Inventor his *Annus Mirabilis*.   He was at this date twenty-five years of age.

There appeared about the year 1887 an article in the *Bristol Times and Mirror* headed " Professor Ericsson and Dr. Edward Hodges, of Bristol," from which article I extract the following :

"SIR :

" I think it will much interest many of your readers to compare the statement made in the slight sketch of the life and work of the Inventor and Scientist, Ericsson, (whose death at the age of 85, has just been telegraphed from New York,) with an extract from the Records left by Dr. Edward Hodges of his own ' Projects and Inventions ' in the field of Mechanical Science.   ' The Screw Propeller,' Ericsson's most important invention, was invented in 1836.   ' The Princeton ' with a Screw propeller was built later.   His last vessel (all this was in New York) was the

'Destroyer,' which carried a sixteen-inch gun, which discharges, with gun-cotton, a 1500 lb.-projectile. In later years Ericsson's attention was given to Solar influences.

"We will now turn to the record left by Dr. Hodges of his 'Inventions and Projects, A.D. 1821,' and quote verbatim.

"'A method of impelling boats (by any mechanical mover) by means of *large screws under water*. Smith (Organ Builder) tells me that Lord Stanhope had the same notion, and had tried it unsuccessfully.

Aug. 8, 1821.'"

On the subject of Explosives, Dr. Hodges writes that he had

"An indistinct notion of applying the moderated, gradual explosion of Gunpowder, as in squibs and sky-rockets, to the impulse of ships. The resisting medium being, of course, the water behind the vessel. Ships so provided might get off faster when chased, and in a calm, might even move with great velocity; but of course at a great expense of powder."

It would be interesting to find out who was the successful projector of "*Sections in Ships*"; but I give Dr. Hodges's words—

"A project for the prevention of the destruction of ships by fire or leakage by means of *Sections* (In bed, Jan. 22, 1821). Wrote S. Gardener Esq. about it. Received his answer Jan. 26. Learned that the scheme had been communicated to several London Merchants, Feb. 4. Result unknown. Appeared in 'Bristol Observer,' March 12. Wrote R. H. Davis, M.P. Received a communication to apply to the Admirality."

Another quotation—

"An Hydraulic Mercurial Steam Engine which may have the same force as the present most powerful engines, yet restricted to perhaps less than an eighth of the space and weight they now occupy."

Strangely too, Dr. Hodges as a lad, was inventing his Photo-meter, and measuring the sun's light, thus directing, like Ericsson, his mind to Solar Influence. He recorded forty-three Inventions and Projects in the year 1821 alone. They go over a great deal of ground : came into his head at all sorts of times and all sorts of places : in Church, in the Commercial Rooms, (one of his favourite resorts in Bristol,) in bed, in his walks and rambles, or in conversation with a friend. Some are quaint and curiously original, showing a wonderful fertility and forecast of practical and mechanical knowledge ; while *all* indicate a degree of observation and thoughtful intelligence, remarkable in one who had barely reached a quarter of century in years ; and who, besides having his time and attention necessarily given to business, was pursuing with extreme diligence his studies in the Science, Practice, Composition and History of Music.

Of the forty-three inventions, seven were for the Organ (*vide* " Improvement of Organs," 1826–1827, *London Musical Magazine and Review*, by Dr. Ed-

ward Hodges); and the Organ of St. James's, Bristol, was the fore-runner of all the large Organs erected in England, as Trinity Organ, New York, was of all afterwards built in the United States. He was, as a Cathedral Organist told the writer, called an "Innovator," in this instance a term of honour. He wrote of his old organ at St. James's, "the Organ is vile !" He lived to see his innovation universally adopted. Whether he received the credit of it is another matter. It did not trouble him much. "He was," said a distinguished Doctor in Music, of Cambridge, "fifty years before his time." He closes his record with this bit of Philosophy :

"As to my projects mechanical, some are good and useful. They must some day come into popular use. And then whether I have the honour of the Invention or not, I shall have the satisfaction of feeling that I deserve it. There are men in the world, who are at this moment heaping up credit on the brains of others. I would not give a straw to be esteemed the inventor of the Steam-Engine itself, unless I had the consciousness of the fact within me."

Here is a Diary Extract :

"From Mr. Samuel Wesley about my Typhus Pedal.

"LONDON, 27 Duke St., Grosvenor Sq.
"*February*, 1819.

"SIR,

"In answer to the favour of your letter, for which I return my thanks, I wish to observe, that your new invention appears to me exceedingly ingenious, and a great increase of grand effect will be produced in the hands of a complete master of Modulation and of the Organ :— but that it is only in such hands that this end is likely to be attained ; how far therefore it is of general utility may possibly be a question, for I am sure I need not inform you that the number of performers who understand the entire management of an organ is comparatively few.

"I beg leave to add that I shall feel most ready to receive any future communication upon the subject you may judge proper to make to

"Sir, Your obliged and obedient servant,

"S. WESLEY.

"To EDWARD HODGES, Esq., Bridge St., Bristol."

The above relates to a contrivance whereby any number of keys may be held down for an indefinite length of time. It has yet, however, never been made public.

In the Diary of this time my Father writes a great deal about his Typhus Pedal. A clerical friend, who knew him not, and yet seemed to regard him, after all these years, as a living presence in the church, has kindly furnished me with the Greek, adding these pleasant words: "Your Father was a good Grecian when he called his "smothered grandeur" pedal, *a Typhus Pedal.*"

Τῦφος, smoke, vapour.

Τύφω, to raise a smoke.

Metaph. *Τυφόμενος* } smouldering, but not yet
Πολεμος } broken out.

Τυφώδης,   like smoke.

The following extracts from the Diary bear on the subject of his inventions :

" Jan. 24th, 1824.

" As I lay awake in bed during the night I cogitated on the matter of tuning Trumpets, etc., when there came into my head the mode of shortening the Tube and consequently of altering the key-note by means of a tube with a stop-cock.

" 25th.

" As usual now with me I lay awake some hours last night, and cogitated about Trumpets, Windmills, etc.   I devised a new combination for raising water in gardens, viz., the appropriation of the Parabolic curved Tube, in connexion with a horizontal windmill, or two, or three of them, one above another, forming a little tower.

" Feb. 2nd.

" *How to describe a spiral.*   This idea pleased me much at the time; it occurred to me in bed, though not for the first time.   Take a Cylinder whose circumference shall be just the distance you wish to have between the lines, then wind a thread round it having a pen and pencil at the end, first fixing it on the paper or board whereon you wish to describe the figure.   Then by keeping the line out firm and marking the surface as you go, *a true* spiral is obtained.

" Feb. 4th.

" I thought of a new method of constructing chimneys and fire-places in a house, by making the fire in the plinth of a large classical column, the column itself carrying the flue."

Particulars are given and drawing made, and drawings are given of the plans he had for improvement in Trombones.

Oct. 13th.

"Both yesterday and to-day I have both amused and stored my mind in some degree by poring over the Encyclopœdia Metropolitana, upon Manufactures and Machines.

"I have an idea of introducing a new process of printing, which may be appropriately called *Papyrography*, as distinguished from Lithography.

"I propose fixing my paper upon wooden blocks, by means of india-rubber varnish, and am sanguine enough to believe that I can manage to *print both sides at the same moment*, which as far as I know has never been attempted by anybody. I am in doubt as the employment whether of *flat blocks* or of *cylinders*, perhaps the latter will be best for *inking* and *watering*. The operation of printing will be more rapid than any yet known. I am delighted with the idea, and hope to apply it to Music. But alas! where are my funds for experiments?"

In the year 1824 my Father records his invention of a *Flying Machine*. He draws it, and gives full details as usual.

Many years afterwards when in New York he spoke in fun, as well as in sober earnest, of his "Flying Pigeon"; proving that the thought of some machine to *move in air* was yet in his mind.

"April, 11th, 1824.

"Amid the multitude of my projects, I know not which to encounter first,
My New Notation,
My Organ Improvements,

My Rocket Ships,   Life saving apparatus.
My Steam Apparatus,
My Musical Publication,
My Double Trombone (to speak a 62 ft. C)
My Double Bass, (to be stopped mechanically).
Besides various musical Compositions, which I
wish to commence or complete ; (The Last Day,
an Oratorio, The Psalms entire, An Anthem
from the Book of Ecclesiastes, Psalm Tunes, a
few hundreds, Accompaniments of various
pieces, Balaam and his Ass,) and Mechanical
Contrivances, which I cannot at the moment
even enumerate, all crowd upon me, and cause
my purpose to lose the name of action.

" Would that I had the capacity that would receive and
retain all kinds of knowledge, and a bodily fame fitted to
endure eternal study."

When anticipating an important Musical performance, he wrote :

" I rely on my past experience, that in time of greatest
need, I have the greatest confidence and the greatest
power.

" Deo juvante."

" Oct. 4th, 1826.

" Heat Engine.

" The last idea I have at present to insert is but half
fledged, and is in fact but an indistinct apprehension of
the possible existence of a law of heat applicable economi-
cally as a source of mechanical power.
" It is known that a great quantity of heat is as it were

suspended or incorporated in our circum-ambient air, and
that much of this heat is given out when the air is suddenly compressed.

"A year or two ago I started one application of this
experiment, viz., a contrivance for boiling water by means
of a forcing syringe.

" Now, however, I am supposing it possible that there
may be some substance (whether solid or fluid matters
not), which, when acted upon by a given heat, may by its
expansion produce or elicit a greater power than would
be required to produce that heat by the means alluded
to, viz., the forcible compression of our atmospheric air.
Were this but the case with water, we might straightway
have a steam engine requiring not the aid of the heat of
fuel.

" But this is too grand a fact not to have been hereto-
fore detected, if fact it be.

" Here, however, let the idea rest for future contemplation.

" I read Shakspeare and Rabelais much of this day."

" Oct. 16th, 1835.

" In Park Street to-day as I proceeded towards Clifton,
I overtook old Mr. George Cumberland, with whom I
strolled and conversed for a full hour.   He is much interested at present about a school for the blind kept by a
man named Lucas, who is also the inventor of a system
whereby the blind can be taught to read readily from
embossed characters of a very simple description.

" I communicated to Mr. Cumberland my plan whereby
many years ago I enabled William Frost (blind) to amuse
himself and friend at a game of Draughts, I having prepared a board whereon the squares were alternately covered with baize.   The men were thin discs and squares of
millboard, covered on both sides with baize."

CLIFTON PARISH CHURCH.

The blind " singing at sight " !

" I also informed him that a few years ago I had formed a design to make an offer of my Musical talent to the Governors of the Asylum for the Blind, intending to endeavour to instruct the inmates in singing from a simple notation of my invention ; but that I had been prevented by the circumstance of their having engaged a paid teacher to sing and play by ear, just as I was concocting my project."

" *Oct. 14, 1836.   10 A.M.*

" Notation for the Blind.

" I give myself as subjects for meditation this morning my proposed new system of Musical Notation for the Blind, and the Papyrographical project."

" *10½ P.M.*

" I did not descend the staircase all day, but kept to my study and amused (!) myself principally with my own meditations. I made a complete scheme of my Notation, and saw my way clearly to a satisfactory accomplishment of that undertaking. In the Papyrographical process I found I could make no further progress without submitting certain points to the test of experiment. That matter therefore stands over."

" Music Modelling and Casting.

" A new idea occurred in the afternoon. This is a scheme for *modelling* music in clay or wax, which could be done with great rapidity, and taking thence a cast in plaster or some harder material, from which to print, as in the Stereotype process.
" This also is worth thinking about, and should be submitted to experiment."

"Fire Extinguishing Project."

"December 5th, 1836.

"An odd idea entered my head as I was dressing my-self this morning.

"It is neither more nor less than a project for extinguishing fire on board ships by the agency of the deadly aerial products of *gunpowder !*

"This must be thought of again.

"If it succeeds (and I confess I see not how it can *fail*, if the access of the other air can be but moderately prevented, for no flame could live in such an atmosphere) it will be a noble thing to employ such an agent upon such a service. Of course the powder must be slowly consumed, not exploded, (which can be easily done with the aid of moisture) and the vapour must be conveyed between decks.

"Two or three barrels of powder methinks would produce enough to fill the area of a large ship."

"Feb. 22nd, 1837.

"In the evening I meditated on my proposed galvanic or electric engine, to supersede the Steam Engine ! and for the first time thought I saw my way clear to a practical application of the principle on which I have so long pondered.

"This and the Piano-forte occupied the evening until a late hour."

"Ship Saving Invention Filched."

"Sept. 29th, 1837.

"I read the papers. Played some fugues upon a noble Piano-forte at C. Hodges's shop; chatted with various friends and others in various places, and at length got home to dinner at four o'clock.

"Before six I was on foot again. I rambled to the Hot-wells, thence across Clifton to Cotham, and so via St. Michael's Hill to the Commercial Rooms again, where I spent nearly two hours in rummaging old files of newspapers for some letters of mine upon an Invention which another has introduced with eclât.

"It relates to the division of the hull of a vessel into compartments. I have written upon the subject to the *Bristol Observer* in 1821, the *Bristol Mirror* in 1825 and in the *Repertory of Patent Inventions*, etc., for 1831, besides having had a correspondence with the Secretary of the Admiralty (then Croker) about it : yet this Mr. Williams is now to have the credit for the Invention.

"In the evening I prosecuted my search for Documents amongst my own papers."

" 30th.

"Still hunting for papers about the Ship-dividing Invention. I found all I wanted. The next consideration is, what to do with them.

"At the Commercial Rooms, Tyson, seeing me, put into my hand a note from himself containing a slip of paper cut out from the *Morning Herald* of yesterday's date.

"It proved to contain a letter from Sir George (or Mr. George) Rennie, claiming the Hull-dividing invention as *his*, struck out about three years ago.

"I subsequently deposited all the documents which I had been collecting at the *Mirror* office, for Tyson's perusal at leisure."

" Oct. 14th.

"An Article (written by Tyson) headed "Safety Steamers" appears in the *Mirror* to-day, justifying my Claim to the priority of invention over Mr. Williams and George Rennie.

"After all there is no probability of pecuniary advantage to me at least, although my inventions may be adopted and my fellow creatures benefitted by them."

It is a matter of gratification, if no more, that at least my Father's invention of *Sections in Ships* is recorded.

" Feb. 12th, 1835.

" At dinner-time an odd notion struck me of constructing a *Sun-dial which should strike* the hour of noon.

" The thing would be easy by the adjustment of a lens, so as to throw the focus of the sun's rays on a thread precisely as the sun attained its meridian."

Sun-dials have always had a peculiar charm and fascination for me. I have often wandered about the Precincts or the Close of a Cathedral, or the Quad. of a College, tracing them out.

They are so unique and suggestive, and have such a voice of Eld ; and they have a way of bringing to mind the idea given to our infantine perceptions that the " Sun was made to rule the day." Then their quaint Mottoes in Latin or Greek ! and their cabalistic characters. It was on one of our perfect English summer afternoons that I was standing, looking up at the Sun-dial on Ely Cathedral. I could read parts of two Greek words I saw there, though the letters were imperfect—suggesting " Gnostic " and " Chronos " yet I could not exactly make out their sense.

The Cloister door opened, and that genial and lovely man, the Archdeacon of Ely came towards me.

He must have noticed that I was puzzled, and looking up at the Sun-dial he said :

"'Know the time.' Good words to keep in one's heart."

Observing his dress—for we were unknown to each other—I asked, "Have I the honour of speaking to a Bishop?" and he said with a kindly smile, "No; only an Archdeacon!"

Then he approached the ivy-draped door of the picturesque old Deanery, opened it, and was gone, and the door was shut.

I stood awhile and pondered on these great words,

KNOWLEDGE and TIME,

and the endless avenues of thought they open out.

I copied the Greek motto, and thought of the Archdeacon's earnest and beaming expression as he interpreted it, and of the fleeting vision of his presence.

Then I stood gazing at the stupendous grandeur of the Cathedral as its Towers and Chapels were brought into light by the rays of the descending sun. I thought of the almost incredible work of the Faithful Monks, whose voices from the very stones seem to say, "Go thou and do likewise!"

14

With a parting glance at the sun-dial, I wandered down the green slope south of the Cathedral, at the foot of which I could distinguish some remains of the monastic buildings. Built on to the end of them I found a *real English cottage.* The garden gate was open. I entered and was welcomed by a pleasant woman who said she was accustomed to furnish tea to strangers. She showed me the old buildings and the garden, and sat chatting about Ely and the Cathedral, as I took tea in her cosy parlour. She mentioned Archdeacon Emery with reverent affection, and I easily saw that my good Greek interpreter was universally beloved.

Then after a moderate payment and many kind words, I wandered out. I saw the river, still flowing on, where the " Monks of Ely sang," and with a parting glance at the noble Cathedral crowning the green hill before me, and a thought for my now vanished friend, the sun-dial, I betook me to mine Inn.

My Father had more than once visited Ely ; and had a great regard for Mr. Skeats, who was Organist there when he took his Degree at Cambridge. Indeed the love and appreciation with which my Father was remembered there, was the source of most of the pleasure I had in visiting this quaint Cathedral town in the Fenlands.

MALMESBURY ABBEY.

CHAPTER XVII.

THOSE who loved my Father would like to know his last acts in music, and the last chords his fingers rested upon. These little facts have a mournful interest ; but I will give them faithfully.

One of the last of his grand services at which I was present, was the Atlantic Cable Celebration at Trinity Church in, I think, 1858.

This was a service of national or international rejoicing, and necessarily differed from a church festival. The city was *en fête*. The British flag, always a delight to my Father's heart, was seen everywere, united with the " Stars and Stripes." Trinity Church had an arch of flowers erected at the chancel steps, under which stood the noble form of the Bishop of New Jersey, the Rt. Rev. George Washington Doane, and thence he delivered a noble oration. My Father played Handel's " Zadok the Priest," and Handel's " God save the King," and never did Trinity organ, made *alive* by its master at the keys, give forth more noble sound.

It was said, and may be mournfully true, that the excitement my dear Father was under on this occasion, together with the tremendous pressure the organ keys demanded, produced the illness which soon after followed, and from which he never fully recovered. I remember one day he asked me, or rather insisted on my trying, to play, and the resistance of the keys was tremendous. It was simply surprising that his hand of sensitive muscles and nerves, not made of iron, had ever mastered it.

There follows a blank to me. It seems as though a shadow had fallen.

I was not in Trinity until some time after, and I know it was not Sunday, for I was below in a pew, and there were not many in the church. My Father was at the organ, and he played his own Kyrie, in E minor. I never heard anything so touching in my life. I cannot describe it. The organ seemed like a human thing in tears. The artistic finish of the perfect musician was so apparent ; and the subdued prayerful plea for mercy was never more present than in the sad soul that organ seemed to possess. I could do nothing but hide down in the pew, and give way to the sadness of that moment.

A Common Metre hymn was given out. The tune my Father played was the one in American books called "Christmas." It is from Händel : " He was eyes unto the blind." It came forth as the Kyrie did, as it were in tears. His own exquisite harmonies to this tune (which in his " Trinity Collection " he called " Vision ") he did not play ; so I think that his own music—the old grand music of Trinity,—having been shut up, was removed by my brother Sebastian and myself, when we found it was not to be continued. Händel's melody was left ; and this came out full of sweetness. But it was all different, all changed, as if the golden bowl was indeed broken, and the silver cord loosed. Händel's melody was finished, Trinity organ knew my Father no more.

His illness necessitating a temporary withdrawal from his position at Trinity Church, he and Mrs. Hodges went to England in 1859 ; but in 1860 we read in a New York paper :

" In a letter to C. Jerome Hopkins, of this city, bearing date November 16, Dr. Edward Hodges, the venerable organist of Trinity Church, who is now in England, says :

" 'It is possible that I may return to New York in the spring ; many circumstances seem to point that way. With the powerful aid promised me by an eminent organist, who now promises to go with me and relieve from the more laborious part of my duties in connection with Trinity Church, and if it please God that my health should continue to mend, I may perhaps resume my old post.

" 'If such should be the case, I am happy to believe that there are not a few warm-hearted friends who would be glad to welcome me once more.' "

My Father returned to New York with Mrs. Hodges, and remained in retirement at Woodlawn, in the Highlands on the Hudson, the residence of her brother, William Moore, Esq., until her death in 1861.

There is another heart-breaking little incident which should not be left amongst the unrecorded, soon forgotten things of life.

I must first premise that when residing in the Highlands he played at St. Philip's Church on a little melodeon, which he called a " short-winded affair," at the Sunday services.

The tone and religious voice he brought from this insignificant little machine were a cause of wonderment to many. At Woodlawn, however, he had a fine-toned Alexandre organ. This he managed to perfection ; it was exceedingly difficult to do justice to its delicacy and power, and sensitive swell. It became under his hand a most beautiful instrument, unmanageable to all but an artist.

Here at her brother's, my second mother lay "sick, even unto death." Devoted to my Father's sacred music, she asked him to play to her "Rock of Ages." He played the fine old Moravian tune in C Minor, to which he always adapted the hymn. It was a supreme moment. Her spirit, borne perhaps on the wings of that music, soon after rose "to worlds unknown."

My Father had closed the organ; he never opened it again. He presented it to St. Philip's Church in the Highlands.

At the Rectory of Grace Church, Newark, the residence of his son, the Rev. J. Sebastian B. Hodges, D.D., my Father spent the last two years of his sojourn in the United States. He finally sailed for England with his son Jubal, June 3, 1863.

It is towards evening. The setting sun-rays light on the steeples and towers of the many churches of Bristol. The weary pilgrim reaches the hills and sees spread before him the old city of his birth and childhood and of the triumphs of his early manhood.

Leaning on the arm of his son Jubal, he reaches the house of his beloved and only sister, Mary.

The family gather in the hall to welcome their revered relative; and as he enters, and ere he receives one word of greeting, his gentle and clear tones are heard in the words of the Christian disciples of old,

"Peace be to this house."

His favourite Fugues—when did he leave them off? I know not exactly, but perhaps when residing at his son's in 1862 or 1863; the effort I witnessed may have been the last. His old Broadwood was there; and I remember how he opened Bach, and essayed to play. His fingers did not obey to his satisfaction, and after trying one Fugue,—and I regret I cannot remember the key, —he said a few words, closed the book, and returned to his seat.

He was a constant reader of good novels at this time, and thus his mind rested; and it was at this time also he said to me that he admired (or liked) "a woman's style for its care in detail and power in drawing character."

When residing at Clifton, it was a great pleasure to him to be drawn in his Bath-chair over to Kingsdown to visit his sister Mary, Mrs. R. H. Webb. We were all gathered in the drawing-room one day and being near the piano, my Father was

CLIFTON CHURCHYARD.

moved to sit down at it.   Instead of improvising much, he began his own tune " Haight."   This he managed well for a verse or two, and at last the old fire kindled; the inspiring occasions when he made his superb, exultant chorus ring through the Church at Christmas, "Shout the glad tidings, Messiah is King," may have flashed across his spirit and he essayed to run up to the E with the freedom of action that used to carry us all along with him; but alas ! the poor hand failed—the eagle's wing was cut—and it could soar no more !

As I stood beside him, hardly keeping back the tears, he looked up in my face, and smiling, with an exceeding sad and plaintive voice he said :

" I used to make a good run there !"

So " Haight" was the last tune he played.   I think he finished it on this occasion ; but I never heard him touch a piano again.

One more scene :

It is September the first, 1866, in his little parlour, where near the window stood a small, good-toned harmonium.   It was placed so that its back rested against the dining-table, and the player sat with back to the window.

My Father again was suddenly moved to play, which I do not remember his having done during the fourteen months I had been with him.

He then arose from his chair and gently helping himself by the table, he walked round it and took his seat at his little harmonium.

He began with his soft, sweet, suggestive modulations, and played a little while in the key of D minor.

Something crossed that sensitive spirit; some whisper reached his ear perhaps: "Not here! not here!" or a voice may have said, "Come up higher!" I know not, but this time he seemed *to realize all.* He gradually finished in his chosen key, and with his left hand slowly followed down the notes of the common chord:

He then arose, and shut down the organ; and as he closed it, said the single word "*Gone!*"

It was that very day the next year, September the first, 1867, that his spirit fled, and I then could bitterly, yet thankfully, realize the meaning of his one word, "Gone!"

He was "translated" as he said.

My Father had a peculiar love for the number

three, and he wound it into many a daily association. His three knocks, three times saying or doing a thing, and (I believe not original with himself) his three coats, " Heightem, tightem, and scrub."

Remarkable it was, that ere he had been also " translated into the world of spirits" twice twelve hours, I happened to glance at the heavens, and there his favourite sign was written : for I instantly saw the three stars, the chief ones, of the Constellation *Aquila*.

Never has my eye lit upon those three stars since, but the memory of that calm September night, with its threefold tone of grandeur, solemnity, and grief, has come back to me afresh : so near me in that bitter realization of the wonderful unbroken repose ; so far from me—the dawning of his immortality !

How Mendelssohn's lovely solo comes floating back to the memory when time, so Divinely ordered, has dulled the edge of grief, " Then shall the righteous shine—shine—as the stars in their heavenly Father's realm."

At early morning, Sunday morning, he left us.
" Let me go ! for the day breaketh ! "

His last words, written with his own hand in his Diary, at Clifton, in July, 1865, were:

" Surely goodness and mercy shall follow me all the days of my life, and I will dwell in the house of the Lord for ever."

CHAPTER XVIII.

THE CHURCHYARD AT STANTON DREW.

" Eye hath not seen, ear hath not heard, neither have entered into the heart of man the things which GOD hath prepared for them that love Him."

" THE retired village of Stanton Drew in this neighbourhood was, on Friday last, the scene of a solemnity of somewhat more than usual impressiveness, on the occasion of the funeral of the late Dr. Hodges, several of whose ancestors lie in the burial-ground of its Church. There is always something peculiarly touching when one, long separated from early connections, who has achieved reputation in the course of a life, is brought, perchance, from distant regions, to join them in the ancestral grave. But in this case the feeling was heightened by the additional circumstance that, as a tribute of respect to the memory of the deceased and to the high rank he held in the musical profession, all the lay-vicars or clerks of the Cathedral who could attend, acting on the kind suggestion of Mr. Corfe, handsomely volunteered to sing to the

Composer's own music those portions of the solemn ritual of the dead appointed to be thus rendered. The other parts of the service were most impressively read by the Rev. Robert Taylor, of Norton-Malreward, and the Rev. Dr. E. A. Hoffman, of New York : the first an old friend, at St. James's Church, Bristol, at the time its organ was in charge of Dr. Hodges; the other, his intimate acquaintance on the other side of the Atlantic, one who knows better than any one living how highly he was esteemed in the United States.

" Nothing could have been more appropriate or opportune, as Dr. Hoffman only arrived by accident in this country just at the time of Dr. Hodges' decease, and was thus enabled, by taking part in the ceremony, to represent that large body of Trans-Atlantic friends, whom it has been his good fortune to attach to himself during his residence among them.

" The 90th Psalm was admirably chanted by six of the gentlemen of the Cathedral and six boys, at the opening of the service, while the corpse rested within the sacred edifice ; followed at the grave in the part assigned to it, by ' I heard a voice from Heaven,' set to music by the deceased, a composition of the most exquisite pathos, and which must have sent a thrill through the breasts

INTERIOR OF ST. MARY'S CHURCH, STANTON DREW.

of all present, given as it was with the greatest precision and delicacy by such an able band of singers. At the close, and following the Benediction, Bach's Chorale from his 'Passion Music,' No. 97, 'O Sacred Head now wounded'; and the friends of the deceased moved away deeply impressed and affected by a solemnity, such as was perhaps never witnessed before in this secluded village district.

" There, in the Druid's Stone Town, by the side of those remarkable remnants of primitive, religious or judicious Institutions, under the shadow of hills on whose summits lie entombed, in their peculiar fashion, the Pagan aborigines who here met in conclave—where curiosity or love of antiquarian research still attracts our modern wandering sages —lies, deposited with Christian rites, one whose connection with this hill-embosomed spot will add to it a further interest, different in kind from theirs.

" The Christian Church and Pagan Temple, still wearing their own characteristic forms, the expression of two eras in human progress, one of which is separated from the present moment by the whole range of history, while the same sun and unchanging hills and groves still illumine or cast their shadows around the place in its perfect isolation, here occupy the same site.

" Nothing but the speechless stones of the one remain ; but the other will still tell to unborn ages its message of mercy ; and the voice of him whose mortal remains have just been committed to its keeping, will continue to speak in many a joyous and devout cadence of sacred song, though no longer in the body.

" It would be impossible in such a place and on such an occasion that the mind should not be forcibly arrested by thoughts such as these, in part suggested by the picturesqueness and hoar antiquity of the surrounding accompaniments ; and we offer this apology for something more than the trivial notice of a good man's obsequies."

(From the pen of my Father's learned, esteemed, and affectionate friend, Alfred Day, Esq., LL.D., in the Bristol *Times and Mirror*, September 6, 1867.)

It is the 6th of September, 1867.

A very quiet and unpretending funeral procession of a hearse and two or three black coaches was seen passing along the shaded, villa-lined roads of Clifton.   It went by the Cathedral, and through the somewhat narrow and tortuous streets of old Bristol ; the very scenes of his childhood and early manhood. It passed out of the city, and followed the road that crossed the Dundry range of hills lying southward of it. It wound its way for seven or eight miles along the smooth turnpike road, and through quiet villages as they came ; when turning to the right it entered a narrower, tree-shaded lane with its high, thick hedges, and here and there, a lonely, rural, and very English thatched cottage. It crossed the little winding river Chew by its gothic, stone-arched bridge, and soon reached the Church of St. Mary, whose ancient tower had appeared above the trees ; while from it there came, at intervals, the slow sound of its tolling bell.

There were farm-yards, and hay-ricks ; and the cottagers, as they heard the horses' feet, came to their doors to see.

It was here, to this quiet village churchyard, that my dear Father wished to be carried. And in the fact of its being his wish—his patriarchal wish we may say,—to be carried back and "buried with his fathers," the vein of sentiment and poetry running through his nature is very apparent, and is most touchingly alluded to in the heartfelt words of his friend Dr. Alfred Day, in his appended obituary notice. It seems that here and here only was the fitting place for his final rest.

If he stood near the very place at the burial of

his aunt, Elizabeth Hodges, in September, 1834, as
I feel almost sure in my own mind he did,—though
I have but memory to refer to,—the thought of
that quiet ancestral spot as his own resting place,
may have received further fixedness in his mind.

It is very quiet there! The birds sing, the rain
falls gently on the many grass-grown graves and
crumbling tombstones. The sun comes up behind the eastern aisles and gables of the church
close by; and there are few trees to interrupt the
broad sheen of light that falls around until the
evening shadows come.

The pensiveness of the poet Gray's spirit might
well have been his, as his eye fell either on the rich
spread of country around, or on the crumbling
stones at his feet, with their letters all erased or
moss-grown, and realized that here his own "fore-
fathers slept." It was his habit to moralize, as he
did some years before when, wandering in Egham
Churchyard, he saw "divers wooden tombstones.
At first" (he says) "I smiled at the folly of the
parties concerned in this *Timber immortality;* but
reflection repressed my laughter. All our monuments in turn have crumbled, do crumble, and will
crumble to dust, be they of what material they may.
Why then laugh at the wooden tombstone? Mine
be of paper, or still more frail material."

STANTON DREW.

But to return.   A low wall runs around the churchyard; ivies and evergreens were there in plenty; but it was not adorned with flower beds, nor had it well-kept graves with floral tokens on them.   All these, with many other signs of life and care, have come in the present good Vicar's time.   It had an air of age and neglect; still it was very peaceful and sequestered.   Up the lane come the wagons close to the gate and the hay-makers' voices are heard from the farm-yard close by, and the merry tones of children at their play. But the busy world, with its toil and struggle and unrest, is not there.   The bell from the old tower at intervals breaks the silence, and the village folk come up to church to prayers.

It is as he would have it, and it is fitting and right that we should have laid him there.

Requiescat in Pace!

An American gentleman gives this account of a visit to the grave of Dr. Hodges, November 6, 1869.

"I have been on a visit to some friends in the neighbourhood of Bristol.   Among other objects of interest I visited, were the Druidical remains at Stanton Drew.   After inspecting these gigantic

monuments which time has not been able to de-
stroy, although countless centuries have passed
over them, I paid a visit to the village churchyard, where my attention was arrested by a handsome white marble cross, which was the more
conspicuous from its being surrounded by old-fashioned grave-stones, over-grown with lichens, moss,
and other creeping plants.

"Judge of my surprise when on reading the Inscription, I found that it was a memorial of the
distinguished father of an able pastor of your city,
whose church I generally attend when a resident
in Newark. I refer to the Rev. Dr. J. Sebastian
B. Hodges, the deservedly respected Rector of
Grace Church.

"The monument, as I have said before, consists
of a simple Latin cross, which rests on three
blocks of marble. The grave is enclosed in a
handsome stone setting, within which were groups
of scarlet geraniums in full flower, which were evidently cared for by a loving hand. On the arm of
the cross is engraved this passage from Holy
Scripture : 'For the trumpet shall sound and the
dead shall be raised incorruptible.' On the three
blocks below the following :

' Sacred to the Memory of

EDWARD HODGES.

Doctor in Music, of Sydney Sussex College, Cam-

bridge,

who died at Clifton, aged 71 years.

Sometime Organist of St. James' and St. Nicholas'

Churches, Bristol, and for a quarter of a cen-

tury, Director of the Music of Trinity

Church, New York, U. S.

Departed this life on Sunday morning September

1, 1867.

This Monument to an honoured Father is erected

by his four surviving children : Faustina,

Jubal, Sebastian, and Asaph.' "

Three seasons have passed since the death of Dr. Hodges. It is now December 23, 1870, and the grave is opened afresh, and the remains of the beloved Jubal being brought down from London, are laid there also.

A flat stone, round which flowers are planted, bears the following inscription :

" In Loving Memory

Of the Rev. Jubal Hodges, Presbyter in the

Diocese of Pennsylvania, U. S.

Born in Bristol, Aug. 29, 1828, Died in London,

Dec. 15, 1870.

He was a sound Theologian,

A Teacher of the Truth,

A rare Musician,

A man of a gentle and loving spirit,

And a friend of the poor.

' Blessed and holy is he that hath part in the First

Resurrection.'

This stone is placed here to his beloved memory

by his sister Faustina."

The Church of St. Mary, Stanton Drew, Somerset, has been carefully and beautifully restored and chastely decorated under the supervision of the learned and estimable Vicar, the Rev. H. T. Perfect, the Vicar of this Parish and St. John's, Pensford.

Two brass tablets placed in this Church state

ST. MARY'S CHURCH, STANTON DREW.

this fact and also another, viz., that the east or chancel window of this Church of their ancestors has been placed here by Faustina Hasse Hodges, in loving memory of her father and brother sleeping here.

"Until the day break, and the shadows flee away."

CHAPTER XIX.

DISCONNECTED RECOLLECTIONS EXTENDING OVER
MANY YEARS.   SOLDIER AND SERVANT.

MANY are the manifestations throughout my
Father's life of his being the "faithful
servant" of God.   He loved to speak of the Deity
as his "Master," thereby owning His personal care
and guidance ; he loved to speak of "His service"
being "perfect freedom" ; but I find one little
entry in particular that gives to this faithful "service" a grand masculine dignity.   The ring of the
Conqueror's voice is heard above the strife.   The
tone of the trumpet rises above the battle-smoke ;
there may be death, but the last sound will be Victory in this "warfare that knows no discharge."
There are very few words—there is no boast about
them, but they evince what is better, viz., calm
resolution.

Simply recognizing the fact, he says : " No wonder then the Devil tempts me, but by the grace of
God he shall not succeed."   "I have fought him

for many years on this very point ; and it would be a shame to yield to him now."

There were three characteristics of my Father which made it always a pleasure to others to get him to speak his mind, viz. : his kindness, his knowledge, and his perfect honesty. One always got what one wanted from him.

There is a little incident connected with the late Rev. Dr. J. H. Hopkins which proves the above true. Dr. Hopkins, it is well known, composed many tunes and carols for Church use, and early in my Father's life in New York came to him with a bundle of MSS. He was not sure of himself ; and wanting to know the truth he placed the music in my Father's hands and said :

" Doctor, will you please look over these, and tell me if I *know* anything. If I do *not*, please to say, No."

He waited patiently while the kind face bent over his work ; and looking at Mr. Hopkins with his in-telligent, fatherly smile, my Father said distinctly, " *No*."

" Thank you, Doctor : now I will begin to study."

Of course my Father understood that Mr. Hop-kins needed to get a thorough *knowledge of Har-mony before he wrote more.*

My Father was grandly helpful in his *conversation*, on Music. How many lessons he gave unknowingly ! How generous he was to all young people who desired to learn ! Truly he gave of his talent in a princely way.

My Father always attended the Philharmonic Concerts in New York. He was an honorary member of the Society, and was held in high esteem by all the New York musicians. His entrance was always marked, as he went early, and no doubt enjoyed a chat with some of them. As they gathered, each with his " Fiddle " or Flute or Horn or Bass, etc., one looked at my Father and said, " Doctor, where is *your* instrument ?"

Fancy the New York Philharmonic in one of Beethoven's grand Andantes, with Trinity Organ at its back, and Dr. Hodges at the keys !

My Father enjoyed the Symphonies of Beethoven, as rendered by the Philharmonic, intensely, and he always spoke with grief and intense feeling of the sorrows that fell around the latter years of the great Master.

For Haydn he had a great admiration : he said, " His music is not yet duly appreciated."

And with a kindling enthusiasm he always mentioned the grand old Musician's last act : when, as the French Army was approaching in 1809, he arose from his bed to play his national Hymn, " God save the Emperor."

That loyal patriotism awoke a responsive chord in my Father's heart.

For Mozart as a Fugue writer, he had a high estimation ; and it will be noticed that he used often to play the music of " Don Giovanni " in his Bristol home. When in St. John's Church, New York, he frequently used his own " Service in F," which was a favourite. Not knowing whose it was, President N. F. Moore said to him that the harmony of the verse " When Thou hadst overcome the sharpness of death " was singularly like that in the " Statue Scene " in " Don Juan."

It is certainly a powerful passage, and though different in treatment and result from " Don Giovanni," bears some similarity to it. I notice a chord in it which, to my mind, exemplifies my Father's theory of " two Fundamental Basses." This, however, must remain but a supposition. He smiled at the idea of any of his Music for the Church resembling Opera Music.

He early inculcated in us a great respect for books. " Never sit upon a book ; never trig up a piece of furniture with a book, nor make any use of it but that for which it is intended. Do not turn down leaves to mark your place, nor scribble in

them ; nor, when you read, hold them in the middle
and leave thumb marks.   Always note the Author,
and read the Preface."

He had a custom of very finely marking passages, and then noting the page in the covers, adding a few terse remarks.

Thus, one of his books gave double instruction.
It was like following the steps of a leader in a difficult footway.   His mind had a splendid grasp of a
subject.   His knowledge seemed to extend above,
below, and back of it.   If we wanted information
on any point he could place it plainly before us,
the limits of his own mind never erecting a boun-
dary to a subject.   Thus he taught us to *think*.
Such an example and such an encouragement to
reading was an education in itself, and makes the
best school-routine (except for its discipline) fall
into insignificance.

He constantly referred us to the " Encyclopædia
Metropolitana," and if we were at a loss for the
meaning of a word, would say " Turn it out !" and
down came the dictionary.

I must relate his wonderfully wise and gentle
mode of punishing me as a child for disobedience.

The Bishop's Garden was used by the Subsacrist
of the Cathedral ; and one day I saw a saddled
horse grazing there.   My brother George F.

Hodges, with other boys, was going into the garden ; and though I was told by my father not to
go there, (he was out, so that I could not get permission at this time,) I was so tempted by the horse
and the assistance of my brother, that into the garden I went. Years afterwards proved me a fearless
horsewoman, and this was my first attempt.

I was soon mounted (on a man's saddle) and
was enjoying my ride immensely, when not being
able to guide the horse well, he took me under a
large hawthorn tree, and my neck and arms got
terribly scratched by the sharp thorns.

When my Father returned, he summoned me
(or I went) to his study. " What's this ? What
are all these scratches ?" he said, looking at my
disfigured neck and arms, and perhaps face—for I
do not remember.

" I went into the Bishop's Garden, sir, and got
on the horse, and he dragged me under the hawthorn tree."

" Did I not tell you *not* to go into the Bishop's
Garden ?"

" Yes, sir."

" Then you must leave my presence, and not see
me again till those scratches are healed !"

I felt, oh ! worse than Gehazi indeed ! with the
leprosy of sin.

He was *order* himself in every way—in every detail. It was one of his most striking characteristics. How often he quoted to us,

" Order is Heaven's first law."

Once he detected holes in my gloves. I made him laugh by saying : " A token of genius, sir !"

He said, " I would rather see genius manifest itself in some more tidy way."

He used, at his Hudson Street home, often at evening to take down from the shelves some work, and we would gather around him to watch, or sing. Sometimes it was a volume of Haydn's or Mozart's Masses, (in which case he would say " Give me the good old Latin pronunciation,") or Crotch's " Palestine," or Romberg's " Lay of the Bell," Neukomm's " David," etc., etc. One evening when playing from Romberg, he had come, before he was aware, to the part where the bell is tolling for a funeral—the funeral of a wife and mother.

He suddenly closed the book and put it back on the shelf.

Forty years have passed since that little scene took place, yet the very key (F minor) and the chords of that music are impressed on my mind. I understood my Father.

I remember his morning reading ; his step from

his room to his study (he never, except on Sundays, joined his family at the breakfast table) ; the sound of the little bolt as he drew it, for his private devotions.   His Bible was thus his first reading.

After withdrawing the bolt, as regularly followed his daily Fugue, according to the day of the month. This practice he observed in New York, as well as in his old Cloister home, to which my mind so faithfully reverts.   I learned much from standing at his left hand ; and as soon as I was able, he liked me to put in the lower part, as Pedal Bass.

Before playing a piece myself, he told me always to play a Prelude ; to improvise a little, so as to get quite used to the touch of the instrument.   And always to take heed at the *end*, and bring in the final chords well.

" A blunder in the middle is not so important ; while a blunder at the end spoils the whole piece."

One piece of advice which he gave me has lasted me through life : " Never show the people what you cannot do."

Of my organ playing he said, that I could " prepare people's minds for Divine Service."

What I inherited from my Father was of more value than all the acquirement I could gain, indeed it *was all.*

He said " No woman could play the organ."

And in this, as in all else, he was perfectly true and right

He spoke from his own unapproachable summit.

On my shewing him one of my earliest compositions he helped and strengthened me much by these words :

" What is original is not good, and what is good is not original."

Of course he alluded to its being " original " with *me ;* as he afterwards told me that the same thought might be " original " with many people.

Of *marks* in music, he said : " They were not of much consequence. Musicians did not *need* them ; and those who were not musicians, would not *heed* them."

In improvising I think my Father thought it best to " say a good deal in *one* key," rather than change too much.

The graceful melodies which my Father threw into the *Tenor* and *Alto* parts of the tunes he arranged, as well as into his own compositions, are very widely observed. Once I remarked on the Tenor part being very *low :* he said, " I did not wish the Tenor to bawl there." (It was in a prayerful passage.)

Our Father always checked at once any unkind remark of an absent person ; and any quotation of

Scripture for any but a serious purpose. He would not allow those riddles to be repeated which were grounded on Scripture names.

When his two sons were taking Orders he requested there should never be any controversies, arguments, or even conversations upon agitated points (at that time acute), nor the names " High " and " Low " (Church) mentioned.

A daughter of one of the Professors at the General Theological Seminary said to me, " Generally, we hear the Psalter sung ; when Dr. Hodges plays, we hear the *Psalms of David.*"

His " rattling off " a Fugue or two of John Sebastian Bach meant so much ! It meant *mastery*, and it meant that it lived again under his fingers.

It was a grand thing to hear him have a " good rummage " on a piano. The poor thing did its best, but it seemed to shake under his touch as it talked !

And at the organ, a " free improvisation " was indeed a grand thing to hear.

One old-fashioned good " jig " my Father played when, at rare times, he felt full of musical fun. It was in B♭ ; the harmony excellent, the character decisive ; and as he " rattled it off," his eyes would gleam and flash, and his face beam with playful light. O for the sound of it again ! How his left hand rolled out the octave passages! It was capital!

Here are some helpful words of wisdom from my Father, written at the age of twenty-eight.

" Let a man accustom himself to a constant walk with GOD; let him have a continual sense of His Presence Who filleth all things, and the best prayer will be that which ascends spontaneously from his heart, as he walks, as he works, as he reads, as he amuses himself, as he talks, and indeed in every transaction in which he may be engaged. I sometimes have this habit; would to GOD that I had it more generally! *There is no greater preservative from sin.*"

From his Diary.

"*July 18, 1853.*

" Many serious reflections upon the vanity of the world and the brevity of human life pervaded my mind to-day. These were particularly superinduced by some awful sensations occasionally, in my *brain*, (Can a man of my spare habit die of apoplexy?) and by an examination of my Daguerrotypes, showing as they do most unequivocally decided marks of age. The good Lord give me grace to be ready when my appointed time shall come."

"*July 20, 1853.*

" Fifty-seven years old this day! Alas! alas! what have I *done* in all that time? What that can be remembered fifty-seven years hence? Can *every* man of the millions which co-exist upon the earth, attain to celebrity or extensive usefulness? That can scarcely be. The bulk of mankind *must* ever be of the class of the *ignoti*, if not *ignobiles;* and I must be content to be one of *them*. And what odds? What difference (to use a form of speech very common on the other side of the Atlantic), what difference will it make a hundred years hence, whether a man has attained to a distinguished position in this world or not? So all be right for the *great account*, the trumpery affairs of earth are of little consequence. But we must bear with them whilst here, and make the best of them."

My Father's words on another life :

" Were I asked what is the greatest pleasure man is capable of, I should answer ' Anticipation.'

" Every pleasure is greater in expectation than in the enjoyment. How great then the enjoyment of Heaven, where our actual bliss will exceed our present highest expectations, and where new expectations of still higher happiness will be continually generated and realized.

" Is it to be imagined that Heaven is a place of idleness or listlessness? From the contemplation of the structure of my own mind I should imagine *not ;* for I could not be happy in such a state. If we shall be at all like unto our glorious Creator, we shall be wonderful in *working*, though not endued with the attribute of Omnipotence.

" Then the certainty of an everlasting duration will give such a zest to our undertakings as no sublunary being ever yet experienced. Fatigue, sorrow, sin, pain, will cease, and GOD will be glorified in all His creatures. My prayer is to be made useful ; not to be a dead letter, even in this nether world."

CHAPTER XX.

" Trinity Rectory, New York,
" November 6, 1882.

" My dear Miss Hodges :

" Your request, that I should write out and send you such reminiscences of your honored Father as my memory enables me to give you, is one with which I am most happy to comply ; only I fear that the sum of them may amount to but little, and prove of small value.

" Although I was numbered among his enthusiastic admirers, and had the privilege of a most agreeable personal acquaintance with him, yet I was not on terms of such close intimacy as to have opportunities of observing and treasuring up in recollection the multitudinous little traits and individualities which furnish the material for accurate portraiture, still, you shall have what I recall of the days when I knew him ; days when he was in full strength and vigor, and at the summit of his professional reputation and success.

" My recollections go back to the time when I was a student in Columbia College, and when Trinity Parish was my ecclesiastical home. Your Father was connected with that Parish from the year 1839 until his resignation of his office, in June, 1863.

" As a youth I listened with delight and wonder to his music as I heard it in the Parish Church and elsewhere ; and later, when I entered the General Theological Seminary, I had the pleasure of becoming acquainted with the great Master, and of receiving some instruction from him to which I shall presently refer. I will write down, as simply as possible, what occurs to me in relation to him professionally and personally.

" I should not have the effrontery to undertake the part of musical critic in this connection ; I am neither a practised musician nor yet a critic of musicians or music. But, merely as a person of sufficient culture to know what is good, and of sufficient appreciation to feel the power of the divine art, I have a right to bear my non-professional witness. The highest veneration for his great ability, the warmest admiration of their results : these sum up what I would say.

" As years go by, we look more fondly to the past, and what is there often charms us more than the things immediately about us. Without drawing any comparisons, however, I will say that my education in Church music, such as it was, began under him, and that the tastes fostered under the inspiration of his genius have never been essentially changed.

" It was at the Parish Church that we used to hear your Father in his full power. If the organ in that edifice be, as is said to be, one of the noblest in the country,—in some respects indeed, superior to any others,—it is sufficient to say of him, in order to describe him in one word, that in him that magnificent instrument, or aggregation of instruments, found and recognized its master. No hand ever touched those keys, before or since, with greater vigor, with greater delicacy ; none knew more thoroughly what it was, or what it could be made to do. It was wonderful to listen, while he played ; the vast fabric seemed to roll forth broad rivers of sound, deep and full as the sea ; it was, sometimes, as if the flood-gates had been lifted up beneath which unfathomable waters were falling through the space between us and their source. Again, the listener was fain to hold his breath to catch the faintest echoes from the far away.

" As for the harmonies in his compositions and in his numerous original arrangements of the old Church Tunes, they were delicious ; they fed and filled the artistic and religious sense within us; something within vibrated to their strange and massive combinations.

" Times have greatly changed since the days to which I now refer. Trinity Church was far away; not easily accessible ; slimly attended ; one would hardly know it now for the same place. But no man ever had more appreciative listeners than your Father ; and the lovers of art felt amply rewarded in surmounting the difficulties of attending at the services in that distant region, by the delight experienced in the dignity, the gravity, the solemnity of the choral parts of the office.

" I had a dear brother, younger than myself, a charming musician and a man of most cultivated taste. He was one of those who were passionately fond of your Father's playing, and never wearied of listening to it ; he would come home, after a great service at the Church, enthusiastic at what he had heard, and sitting down at the piano-forte, would draw upon his memory and try to give me an idea of the management of certain themes, or the effect of certain passages.

" You need no words of mine to tell you how Dr. Hodges was esteemed in Trinity Parish. Briefly, it might be said, that the Parish Church and its organist appeared to accord entirely; what Trinity

Church, the creation of Richard Upjohn, was to architecture in the United States, the music at Trinity was to other Parishes throughout the country. It will be generally admitted, I think, that, notwithstanding the fact that it was the first great Church erected in our communion in this country, and although others of much larger capacity and of higher pretensions have been built since it was consecrated, none surpasses it to-day, if any equals it, in dignity, stateliness, and grandeur of effect. It is a monument of the ability of the remarkable man who planned and built it, and in no subsequent work did he excel what he did then. Even so, in my judgment, the fame of the old organist has never been exceeded since he left us ; nor has the traditional power of his name and example lost its force. The sense of decorum, the depth and richness of the great schools of musical art, the manliness and strength of the Anglican thought, the grave religiousness, which wise men venerate, still notably mark the order of our services ; nor are our annals disgraced by meretricious shallowness, or namby-pamby nonsense, or the loose and wanton proceedings which charm the vulgar ear. Whatever changes the days may have brought, a Spirit dwells within that fane, to drive off whosoever would violate the sanctity of the place.

MALMESBURY ABBEY.

" I should like, however, to say one thing here, in the hope that I shall find you in sympathy with me, though others decline to view the matter in the same light.   I think, then, that we have lost something in changing the pitch of the organ.   The original pitch was lower than the present ; the effects produced were, to my ear, immeasurably superior, more tender, more sombre, more thoughtful, though, certainly, less brilliant.   The alteration was made in an underhand way, without the knowledge or consent of the authorities of the Parish ; the story is a strange one, which I could not relate without becoming unfairly personal.   But in order to secure the co-operation of an orchestra of string and wind instruments, the pitch was surreptitiously changed, and raised to that adopted by the Philharmonic Society, while the Rector and Vestry-Committee imagined that nothing beyond a much-needed cleaning and some slight repairs were in progress.   Of course you understand that this was done after your Father's connection with the Church had been terminated, by his attack of paralysis ; he was not responsible for it.   I am sorry it was done, and yet in this sentiment I find little sympathy, and am generally regarded, by those to whom I utter complaint, with a mild and pitying wonder.   But I presume that it is because I am not myself in harmony with the noise, shrillness, and self-assertion which, in this generation, appear to be among the main conditions to popularity and success.

" My personal acquaintance with your Father began when I was a student in the Seminary. On the 17th of December, 1851, the Church Choral Society was formed. It had for its object the study of the Cathedral Music of the Church of England, and for its ambition the public performance of a Choral Service, in this city, if, by any fortunate change of affairs, and abatement in prejudices, permission could be obtained to exhibit so fearful and startling an innovation on all uses then known among us. We met for practice in the school building in the rear of St. John's Chapel ; Dr. Hodges was our drill-master, *Choragus* and *Coryphæus*. I cannot tell you how much I enjoyed our evenings, nor how proud I was of taking part in the first public service. It was held on Tuesday in Easter week, April 13, 1852, in Trinity Church, at three o'clock in the afternoon. The Rev. Messrs. Shackelford, Webbe, Elmendorf, and Hopkins officiated, and the responses and choral parts were given by our Society.

" The church was filled to overflowing, and the impression produced was profound. After that it was only a question of time how long it would be till the fulness of our triumph over the fears and dislikes of the crude and untaught people. To your Father belongs a large share in the honors of that memorable occasion.

" I have some most agreeable recollections of evenings spent at his house, where we were always delightfully entertained by his conversation, and made heartily welcome. The talk generally turned on musical themes, or subjects interesting to the theologian, the ecclesiastic, and the artist. Your Father's face, as I remember it, was animated and earnest ; his manners were polished, his eye bright and clear, his air that of a genial and courteous gentleman. His costume gave him the look of a dignitary of the church ; he wore, if I mistake not, a coat of semi-clerical cut and a white cravat ; his hat was of peculiar shape, and ample enough in brim to have passed for that of an Archdeacon at the very least. As to his shoes, I shall never forget them, modelled, apparently on the pattern of a bricklayer's trowel, they ran out to sharp points in front ; and I never could imagine what was the secret of that strange construction, which indeed was unlike anything except the specimens given by Balduinus in his work *De Calceo Antiquo*, or Julius Nigronius de Caliga.   But on enquiry it appeared that he had his shoes in that shape for the more convenient manip-—no, I should say *ped*ipulation of the instrument ; since, in fact, the pedals were arranged like the sticks of an open fan which radiate from a centre ; and the sharp-toed shoes went in and out, and up and down among them in a way which must have been seen to be appreciated.

" His manners had a certain crispness which constituted especial charm for his friends and was not without effect on foes, if he had any ; and his speech was, as it were, full of punctuation marks and notes of emphasis, as became a man who had strong convictions and scrupled not to express them if necessary. Yet there was often in his face an expression which bespoke the profoundly religious spirit. That fine profile portrait of him which you remember and which now hangs in the Vestry Room at the Church is an ideal head ; the face is that of one who, in " beating out his music," meditates of holy themes and seems to hear the voices of another world.

" I remember among other lessons taught me by your Father, one which sank deep into my soul and brought forth fruits of penitence then. On the occasion to which I now refer, I was the victim of the arts of a friend, who, if his eye should ever fall on these words, would no doubt recall his conduct with compunction, and bless my forbearance in not naming him.

"He was an organist, and a most successful choir-master, and among the most intense and enthusiastic admirers and disciples of Dr. Hodges. Whenever he had the good luck to get to New York, his first move was to repair to Trinity and bathe himself all over in the grand music. This man and I being on most intimate terms, and he being desirous of obtaining a copy of your Father's arrangement of 'Luton,' yet not daring to ask for it, conceived the idea of using me as a cat's paw to pull out the coveted chestnut. So he wheedled me into writing a letter to Dr. Hodges, and asking for a copy ; which I did in the innocency of my heart, and the simplicity of my hands. But in due time I got a letter, and such a rating as my temerity deserved ; probably the Doctor suspected the concealed hand, and plied the lash across the shoulders of the real culprit ; informing me that a Musician's compositions were his property and his fortune, that they had a market value, and that it was no joke to be giving away, right and left, what stood for so much capital ; with more to that effect. To comfort me after the discipline, I found enclosed the copy of 'Luton' beautifully written out by your Father, and so exquisitely done as if in copper

plate, with some cordial words, the offset to the
paternal remonstrances in the epistle.   To say that
my astute friend seized on it with avidity, chuckling
over his success, is but to add the inevitable conclusion to the story of the way in which he played upon
my inexperience.   But we both enjoyed the harmonies, as if nothing adverse had been encountered
in the manner of their acquisition.

" I came to Trinity Church in the year 1855.
Among the clergy was the Rev. J. F. Young, then
a Junior Assistant Minister, and now Bishop of
Florida, who, not content with thoroughly appreci-
ating your Father's powers and greatly admiring
his art, was ready to unite with me in an attempt
to induce him to publish some of those compositions
which were chief favorites among our people.   One
difficulty in the way was this, that Dr. Hodges insisted on using the old Tenor and Alto clefs, and
would not demean his work by printing it in the
ordinary manner.   Nothing would induce him to
recede from his position, so we swallowed the clefs,
and got several of his services into print.   The first
thus published, A. D. 1859, was the ' Communion
Service in F ' which has a preface that tells the story
in his own words, as follows :

" ' This Service was written in the year 1843.   It
has been for some time in ordinary use at Trinity

Church New York, and is now published at the
particular request of two of the clergymen connected with that Parish, the Rev. Morgan Dix,
M.A., and the Rev. J. F. Young, M.A.

"'Such a request, backed as it was by the voluntary undertaking of those gentlemen to purchase
a considerable number of copies, could not well be
refused ; so the score was taken from the conceal-
ment in which it had lain for fifteen years, and after
having been fairly copied by my good friend and
disciple, Mr. W. H. Walter, Organist of Trinity
Chapel, at a time when severe illness compelled me
to cease from all professional labours, was committed to the printer.

" ' Still sequestered from active duty, and uncer-
tain whether my recovery will ever be such as to
qualify me to resume it, it will be a source of high
and holy gratification to learn that my humble
strains contribute in any degree to aid the devotions
of the Christian Church.'

" The 'Evening Service in C,' composed in 1824,
was published in 1863, under the supervision of
Dr. Walter; and the wonderfully beautiful Anthem,
written for the Consecration of Trinity Chapel in
1855, must have appeared some years later. I think
that those three works are enough, by themselves,
to establish the position of your Father, as that of

one of the ablest, purest, and most delightful of our
Church composers, and to set him on high among
the masters of the Anglican School.

" Mention ought also to be made of his skill and
success as a writer of English prose. His style
was finished, and his acquaintance with the resources of our native tongue sufficient to make his
compositions most agreeable and acceptable to persons of cultivated taste. He was especially clever
in humorous and good-naturedly satirical work,
treating his themes with skill and showing a keen
relish of fun and a refined wit. During the great
uproar and assault on Trinity Church in the year
1857, he made a notable contribution to the defence
in the shape of a most effective and amusing pamphlet, entitled, ' Mrs. Trin and her Troubles : A
Parable.'

" Thus, dear Miss Hodges, have I complied with
your request, writing in too great a hurry to revise
what I must now send to you just as it is.

" Your statement in your letter of the 12th
ulto.—' do not think that I want a learned article
for a paper,' emboldens me to offer you, without
apology for its crudeness, the imperfect but sincere
tribute to the memory of one of the most accomplished musicians and most worthy and agreeable
men I have ever had the good fortune to meet.   I

can only say that I wish I had known him better.
There are those who can paint his picture with the
breadth and strength which the subject demands ;
I am satisfied if you tell me that I have succeeded
in contributing a few touches, before its completion
by the proper hand.

     "I remain,

          "With sincere regard and esteem,

            "Very faithfully yours,

                  "MORGAN DIX."

"MISS FAUSTINA H. HODGES."

17

CHAPTER XXI.

From the Rev. Dr. J. H. Hopkins.

" *Williamsport, Pa., July 3, 1885.*

" My dear Miss Hodges :

" My first personal acquaintance with your honored Father was in the autumn or early winter of 1846. I had heard him on the Organ at St. John's Chapel as far back as 1840, for a few months; but at that time had not ventured to speak to him.

" In 1846 I had finished the arrangement of my Father's Church Music—covering a complete body of music for Chants, Psalms, Hymns, and some Anthems. This had been a favorite work with him for more than twenty years, his natural gift for music, and especially for melody, being very great. But he had never studied harmony, and always said he would wait for me to do that part for him. I had accordingly arranged the whole, filling up a few gaps myself; and then, when the bulky volumes of

MS. were ready for the printer, taking them with me to New York in search of a publisher, I thought it only prudent—though I knew it was rather impertinent—to introduce myself to your Father, then the acknowledged head and indisputable chief of Church Music in this country, to *ask* his judgment on the book first. At his request I left the volumes with him for a few days, and on calling again, found that he was too gentle and tender-hearted to say anything that would wound my feelings ; but after a great deal of instructive talk from him, showing the variety, and breadth, and depth of the true Church style, I instinctively *absorbed* the impression that I should not be likely to find a publisher who would take the risk ; and also, that an entire collection produced in such a way would not be of so much service to the Church as I had supposed. No one, even of the greatest Masters of Church Music had ever produced more than a few Hymn Tunes ; and this rule was not likely to be reversed in the case of persons who, during their whole lives, had been beyond the reach of the best music in any school. But this conclusion was impressed so gently, so indirectly, so learnedly, that I admired and loved him for it ever after.

" When I became a Candidate for Orders in the Diocese of New York in 1847 I attached myself to

Trinity Church, and every Sunday walked the three miles down town, getting lunch at some restaurant at one o'clock, and walking back after Evening Service. The greatest inducement for me to attend there was the music, and your Father's wonderful organ playing. Of the sermons I heard there I do not remember much. But the music was another thing! The subdued and reverential tone of the opening voluntary, was a fit preface for the General Confession and the Lord's Prayer. The 'giving out' of the Hymn Tunes was an exquisite treat ;—the melody being played on a rich and peculiar combination of stops on the Swell Organ, while the accompaniment was on another manual. The *feeling* that was thus embodied is indescribable in words. The striking character of the accompaniment to the voices, the interludes —especially, for instance, in Luther's Judgment Hymn (commonly so called)—testified to the religious and real character of the whole. His Church playing was always an act of worship. How many of those grand Hymns ring in my memory yet! 'What are these in bright array,' 'Rise crowned with light,' 'Although the vine its fruit deny'; Bristol, Peace, Manchester, St. Ann's, the Old Hundredth, and so many others. I shall never hear them done in that glorious style again! The

Cathedral Services, which were commonly given for the Canticles, in both Morning and Evening Prayer, together with the Anthems, which came more rarely, were of the highest range in purity of taste and distinctness of character. But to me the crown of them all was his own 'Consecration Service,' which was a special joy whenever I could hear it. The closing movement of the 'Te Deum" in that Service, taken up again and further expanded at the close of the Benedictus, is the grandest thing I know in the whole circle of Cathedral Services. The great waves of sound follow one another like the ocean swells in regular movement round the curved shore, until they die away in the distance. They always gave me a peculiar thrill of delight. And at the close, after the Benediction, the grand voluntary was always an invitation to make me stop, until the last note was silent. I would sooner have gone out in the midst of the sermon than of that voluntary. The religious grandeur of the style,—the way in which by constant 'substitution' the fingering was so managed, that the notes glided and rolled and swelled into one another without mechanical breaks, giving the organ a voice as if it were a conscious living creature and not a piece of mechanism—this was the peculiar charm of *his* playing,

which I have never heard in like measure from any
other.

" During all the period of your Father's subsequent sojourn in New York, our friendship continued unbroken, unabated, and unshaded by the
slightest cloud. He was the life and soul of our
' Church Choral Society,' which, under his patient
and thorough training, got up the first full Choral
Service ever sung in this country. And when did
he *ever* refuse or fail to instruct or help those who
came to him for information or guidance in his
noble Art ?

" In the course of those years, in walking up town
to my lodgings, I generally took my way through
Hudson Street. And at nine o'clock in the evening,
or a little later, passing his modest house below
Canal Street, I would enter for a chat with him.
With unvarying regularity, at that time, I would
find him at the centre table in his parlor with his
big Diary before him (it was about the size of a
merchant's ledger) writing up the entries for the
day.

" The inkstand out of which he wrote was a
quaint and grotesque piece of drollery which seemed
to give him special pleasure. When the big book
was closed, some English ale, with ' crackers '[1] and

<hr>

[1] Biscuit.

cheese were brought in, and an hour—sometimes two hours or more—passed away in the most delightful manner.

"One thing remarkable about Dr. Hodges was his thorough theological appreciation of the true meaning of the words and phrases which he set to music. He was a well-read theologian outside of his own professional range, and his communications in the Church papers often showed that he was more than a match for some of the clergy! Still water runs deep! One who saw only the placid, gentle, equable tenor of his daily life and conversation, would not dream that he was capable of the deepest feeling, the most intense suffering, the most enduring affection, the most corroding remembrances. Yet all this was so, though no word of it escaped so as to be observed by ordinary acquaintances.

"The deep undertone of *intense reality* pervaded his whole being, and alas! in some respects, the shades grew only deeper and darker towards the latter part of his abode among us. But *I* saw only the sunshine; and that sweet sunshine has left the memory of its brightness undimmed in the heart of

"Yr. ob. servant in the Church,

"J. H. HOPKINS.

"Miss Faustina H. Hodges."

From the Very Rev. Dean Hoffman.

"General Theological Seminary,
"*New York, January 5, 1895.*

"My dear Miss Hodges:

"My earliest recollection of your Father dates back to the time when he first came to this country, and, through the Rev. Dr. Wainwright's influence, was appointed organist of St. John's Chapel, where I was then attending church. Up to that date Anglican Church music was almost unknown on this side of the Atlantic. The singing of the psalms in metre and one of the small collection of hymns printed with the Prayer Book was, as a rule, the only musical part of the Church service. His handling of the organ with such singular power, and his devotional rendering of the canticles and occasional anthems attracted large numbers to the Chapel, and its influence immediately began to be felt in other churches, lifting the musical portion of the services to a higher and more sacred plane.

"When Trinity Church was rebuilt, at a later day, he was naturally promoted to it. This gave him a wider field and greater influence. The organ there, which was built under his immediate supervision, was at that time the largest and best

ST. MARY'S CHURCH, STANTON DREW.

in this country.   Under his manipulation it seemed to speak, and to give a deeper and fuller meaning to the sacred words.   I have heard members of that congregation say that the words of the hymns or of the anthem, with his musical interpretation of them, left often a deeper impression on their minds than the most eloquent sermon.   His voluntaries at the close of the service, improvisations of his own, were so popular that it was not unusual for a large portion of the congregation to remain in their pews until he had finished.   Though I have heard not a few of the noted organists of England, I have never heard one who surpassed him in devotional rendering of the organ accompaniments.   Under his hand the organ seemed to adapt itself to the various expressions of penitence or praise in the psalms or anthems.

"It was my privilege, as you know, to commit his remains, 'earth to earth,' in the quiet churchyard of Stanton Drew, and I esteem it a duty to express my obligation to one to whom, in common with so many others, I owe my intelligent appreciation of true Church music.

"Very sincerely yours,

"E. A. HOFFMAN.

"MISS FAUSTINA HASSE HODGES."

From the Rev. J. H. H. De Mille.

" The writer looks back to the days of his acquaintance with Dr. Hodges and remembers a genial, elderly man, dignified but full of humour, always seeming to carry with him the impression that his high art was a gift received from Heaven, and therefore to be consecrated to the Glory of God.

" To his work he not only brought a cultivated mind and true musical taste, but deep religious feeling ; and it is not therefore surprising that his compositions are pervaded by a highly devotional spirit. His playing of the organ was remarkable for the same devotional spirit. The writer has again and again seen him as he presided at the Organ of Trinity Church, endeavouring to develop musical thoughts suggested by the sermons to which he gave thoughtful and critical attention. On one occasion the sermon was particularly impressive ; and as the sun, nearing the west, threw a rich light through the stained glass window of old Trinity, he wove the thoughts of the sermon and the rich scene into his concluding voluntary, basing it on the theme of Tallis's Evening Hymn.

" Though twenty years have passed since then, the strains of that music still linger in our memory.

"J. H. H. De Mille."

Sir Frederick Gore Ouseley, Bart., wrote me that he had hurried to Bristol purposely to see my Father and to hear him at his organ with the magnificent swell; and was much disappointed to find that Dr. Hodges had just left for New York.

In another letter to the writer dated October 18, 1887, Sir Frederick says,

"I possess a complete set of the old *Musical Quarterly Review*, and know well your Father's Essays and Letters therein. They were in advance of their period, and display much clever insight into matters of which contemporary musicians were mostly in utter ignorance.

"I wish I had had the good fortune of knowing him personally."

An article in the *Bristol Mirror*, 1867, speaking of his residence in New York after his sojourn there was over, says :

"And in that far Western land he was honoured and respected as the good old English Doctor.

"He never lost his nationality : but having finished his work, he returned under his own flag to the land he loved with the passionate loyalty of an Englishman.

"Homeward bound at last ! Many now in Clifton remember him, as he was drawn about in his Bath-chair, for illness and over brain work had prostrated his powers. They will remember his genial and benevolent countenance, illuminated as it always was with his bright intelligence and sparkling humour. He was truly a Christian Philosopher; and one who gazed upon his thoughtful face with the marks,—light ones in truth—of seventy years upon it, would carry away the impression of one who had done his work well; who had borne his share of life's sorrows bravely; who had consecrated his talents to a noble use, and had come to the end of his journey with the light of a brighter world shining on his pathway."

CHAPTER XXII.

IN MEMORIAM.   TESTIMONY TO HIS WORTH FROM VARI-
OUS JOURNALS.

From the *Church Journal*, New York.

" DR. EDWARD HODGES, whose death was announced
in a recent issue, will long be remembered in this country,
not only as a most accomplished musician, but as one to
whom we are indebted for the best school of our Church
music.   Born and brought up in Bristol, England, the
Cathedral of which has long been noted for its choral
services, and deeply imbued with the spirit of the old
masters, he came to this country at a period when good
ecclesiastical music was but little known in our churches.
His position as organist of old Trinity, afforded him an excellent opportunity for the exercise of his unusual ability,
and his influence was soon felt throughout the Church.
Strangers visiting the city would often make it a point to
remain over Sunday that they might hear the Doctor play.
And who that once heard him can ever forget the power
which he possessed at the organ?   The listener felt at
once that he was in the presence of a master of that
noblest instrument, and a master who realized that its
office in the sanctuary was for God's praise and not for
man's display.   The simple voluntary with which he

would introduce the service, was always a fitting prelude
to prayer, hushing worldly thoughts, lifting the soul from
earth, and giving it the foretaste of celestial melody.
And as the service proceeded and the organ gave out its
utmost grandeur in response to his masterly touch, now
uttering a plea for mercy, now subdued as by the very
presence of THE ETERNAL, and now rolling out the
majesty of praise, there was something which made the
worshipper forget the instrument and the place, and lifted
him, as it were, to the harmonies of the Temple which is
above.   No music was common in his hands.   The organ,
with its delicate mechanism, rich combinations and wonderful resources, was all at his command.   It seemed to
breathe his inmost spirit.   A plain psalm tune would with
him often roll out like a grand Chorale, and when the
service was closed, how often have we heard him take a
simple subject, perhaps suggested by some thought in the
sermon, and after a solemn introduction, give it out and
make upon it a most wonderful improvisation of a Fugue.

" But above all rose his beautiful Christian character.
He lived as though he realized that he was ever in God's
presence.   God's word was his daily study; the life that
was in Jesus his constant pattern.   How promptly he
would hush a word of complaint against anyone; how
gently and delicately he dealt with his choir; how largely
he gave of his limited means to every charity; how carefully he would follow all the responses in the service; how
regularly he knelt at the Altar-rail in the days of his
power amongst us, after having lifted our souls above
these scenes by his glorious rendering of his own setting
of the ' Ter Sanctus,' is well known to all that had the
privilege of his friendship, or perhaps the even greater
privilege of hearing him constantly at the organ.

" When compelled by illness to relinquish his post at
Trinity, he returned to his native city to spend the bal-

ance of his days, and there most peaceful and beautiful was his decline. It was like the evening glow of a bright, well spent day. Undisturbed by a single murmur, as one power after another gave way, with Christian resignation he fell asleep in perfect peace.

" By his own directions, his remains were laid beside those of his ancestors in the quiet Churchyard of Stanton Drew: and nothing could have been more touchingly beautiful than the funeral service in that little antiquated village Sanctuary, which stands near the great stones of an old Druidical Circle or Temple. There was no organ heard; but selections of his own compositions, consisting of his solemn chant in C sharp minor, (written many years previously for that occasion,) and his own funeral verse 'I heard a Voice,' were perfectly rendered by members of the Cathedral Choir, surpliced, as is their custom.

"And as the strains of the Anthem, a composition of exquisite pathos, rose around the grave immediately after the committal, it seemed like the voice of the departed coming forth from the tomb to comfort the mourners. The service was closed with Bach's beautiful Chorale, 'O sacred Head now wounded,' and as the muffled bells gave forth their solemn peal, the friends left the spot more deeply impressed than ever with the great truth,

" 'Blessed are the dead who die in the Lord.' "

Dr. Alfred Day, whose eloquent and feeling account of the funeral at Stanton Drew we have already seen, gave at the same time a description of my Father's personality and characteristics, which seems to make us almost acquainted with him ; and which is valuable as the last we can receive from the hand of any who knew and loved him in Bristol. I shall quote from it so as to avoid repetition.

From the *Bristol Times and Mirror*, Sept., 1867.

"The Late Dr. Edward Hodges.

"This Eminent Composer and Musician died at Clifton on Sunday morning last. Dr. Hodges was well known as a public character in this his native city, a quarter of a century ago; and was admired for his conversational powers, his varied acquirements, and more particularly for his profound knowledge of the theory and practice of Music. Though destined by his father for business, he had no sooner attained to freedom of action, than his peculiar bent and genius developed itself in the direction in which he was afterwards famous.

"Fertile in mechanical expedients, he applied himself with great zeal and energy to the study of the construction of the organ, with marked success; and before many years had become the chief authority on that instrument in Bristol, being consulted on every occasion where an organ was to be repaired or built. He was equally distinguished as a skillful performer on this his favourite instrument, and was also a devoted student of the works of Handel, Bach, Haydn, and Mozart, and our old Church writers.

"Having entered himself at Cambridge, during the Professorate of Dr. Clark-Whitfeld, he obtained the degree of Mus. Doc. at a time when this distinction was rare, after an Exercise which was pronounced to be of unusual merit. He afterwards enjoyed the intimacy of many celebrated musical writers, and among others of the late Samuel Wesley, who has left it on record that Dr. Hodges was one of the first, if not the first, of English organists. Possibly, personal friendship and a sense of personal obligation may have had a share in dictating so comprehensive a statement, but there is no doubt whatever that the Doctor's powers as an extemporary Fugue

UNIVERSITY CHURCH, CAMBRIDGE.

player, and his command and knowledge of the resources of his instrument were of a remarkable kind. No man ever better understood how to adapt himself readily to the frame of feeling in which a congregation of worshipping people might happen to be, or to the exigencies of metre, or the requirements imposed by the tone and sentiment of the words to be sung at particular times and seasons. The writer has known him during service compose original chants or tunes to meet some unlooked-for emergency; and on one occasion of a public nature, when suddenly deserted by his choir, improvise a voluntary which bridged over the gap caused thereby, without the congregation becoming aware of what had taken place. During the period of his presidency at the organ of St. James (which was for many years the best in Bristol, and re-constructed with his specification and oversight) he composed several services, some of which have obtained a permanent place in Cathedral Choirs; and many printed collections of tunes and chants contain well-known specimens of his writing or adaptation.

" For many years Dr. Hodges contributed papers to various journals on Mechanical Science. Among others of his suggestions were the damming of the Avon at Sea Mills, and a scheme for floating the *Great Britain* when on shore in Dundrum Bay. He had also constructed and described a model of a feathering steam paddle-wheel, identical in principal with that afterwards patented as ' Morgan's Paddle-wheel.' Many improvements in the mode of constructing the Swell box and Pedal board of the organ, and other mechanical appliances have been adopted from him.

" Later in life Dr. Hodges was induced to settle in New York, U. S., where his eminent abilities were soon appreciated, and where he may be said to have created a taste for Church music. Under his direction a magnificent organ was constructed for the noble Trinity Church in that city, the musical services of which he continued to conduct for many years with great reputation. We extract the following notice of the proposed publication of the *Te Deum* composed by him on the occasion of the consecration of that Church from a New York paper:

"'Hodges in E.—We are glad to announce what we have desired for years, and that is that the *chef d'œuvre* of Dr. Hodges, written for the consecration service of Trinity Church in 1846 and annually used thereafter on Ascension Day as long as its author was able to preside at the organ, is about to be published. It consists of an opening sentence, the *Te Deum and Benedictus*. All these will be given, not only for the voices, but with separate *obligato* organ part, just as it used to be played by Dr. Hodges himself. And who that has ever heard, can ever forget the chaste yet sublime richness of the drapery, which, in that admirable service, clothes the body of vocal harmony as with the ornament of royal robes? That service, in our opinion, stands at the head of all Cathedral services, as combining a full and overpowering poetic colouring and sentiment, without in any respect departing from the sobriety and dignity of a pure ecclesiastical style; and of all that Dr. Hodges has done for the noble cause of Church music among us, *that* will live the longest and be the most dearly cherished; especially the magnificent close of the *Te Deum* and the *Benedictus*, in which one seems to hear the rolling of the musical waves upon the everlasting shore.'

" This service has since been published with an admirable likeness of the author attached. Dr. Hodges was the first cousin of the eminent sculptor, Edward Hodges Baily, so lately removed by death, and both cherished a high and mutual esteem for each other. Bristol may well be proud of a family which has evinced remarkable talent in many of its members, and has been equally distinguished for its high moral tone. The upper portion of Dr. Hodges' head and eyes reminded one strongly of Mendelssohn. His wit and pleasantry and social qualities were of a high order, and in the old time of Corporation dinners, he regularly found his place at the civic feasts, though himself the most abstemious of eaters. Being of a delicate constitution and very susceptible nervous organization, his health was always precarious, and this will account for his almost premature decay at an age when many continue vigorous, though he had reached the allotted term of human life. During his residence in New York he married the sister of Dr. N. F. Moore, formerly President and Greek Professor of Columbia College, himself a considerable traveller and author, and a most cultivated man. After her death, he returned to take up his residence permanently at Clifton, but was no longer able to indulge his favourite studies from increasing infirmity, or rather mere bodily weakness.

" His last moments were soothed by the unremitting attentions of his daughter, who tended him with the most affectionate assiduity. We have had occasion lately to notice favourably several of her musical productions, and are assured that they display considerable talent, both in the art of composition and in respect of melody, by those more competent to judge than we are. Dr. Hodges' failing strength since his return to England has prevented his being as well known to contemporaries as he was twenty-five years ago to his fellow-citizens of that date. His decay was gradual and peaceful, though at the last somewhat sudden. He was a devout and consistent Churchman, zealous for the extension of Church Music, and worked with one all-absorbing aim in his vocation. He could scarcely be regarded as one who followed music as a profession, certainly not if the idea of pecuniary gain is

involved in the distinction. He rather regarded his art as
something to be dedicated to the service of the Sanctuary,
and himself not as the organist of this or that parish, but
as a liturgical minister of the Church universal on earth.
To render more expressively, devoutly, and grandly its
daily service of prayer and thanksgiving he would have
made any personal sacrifice consistent with Christian duty.
The few surviving friends of his early life will always
cherish his memory with profound regard, and the announcement of his decease will be received with deep
regret by a host of admirers on the other side of the Atlantic, who will associate his name and that of Church
Music indissolubly. Already the MS. tunes and portions
of services left by Dr. Hodges in the Choir books of
Trinity, have found their way into print, and many of
these will be spread far and wide in the future progress
of Church extension in America. At home the use
of *Mercer*, and *Hymns Ancient and Modern*, with the
crowd of rival productions that find favour in different
congregations, stands in the way of any wide adoption of
a foreign selection, but we should be glad to see an entire
selection of all that Dr. Hodges has written thoughtfully
and earnestly in the day of his power, for he has left behind him a valuable legacy in the shape of occasional
Anthems, Morning and Evening Services, and indited
Compositions, which might be brought together, and
would vindicate his reputation as a composer, which is
less known than it deserves to be out of the circle of
his admiring personal friends."

I make rather amusing extracts from an article in
the New York *Keynote*, signed G. F. D., a writer
to me unknown.

" Many New Yorkers of musical proclivities who are
now fairly advanced in middle age, remember Dr. Edward

Hodges, who was for many years organist of Trinity Church in this city.

"The Doctor was an oddity in many ways. One of the greatest Contrapuntists of his day, he was yet very fond of taking simple melodies and passing them through the alembic of his own musical fire, bringing them out so that there was a remote sensation of having heard what you listened to somewhere, but the original theme was so artistically treated that one was at a loss to recognize it, and it gave the general effect of a musical dream, with a suggestion of solid harmony to strengthen it. One of these curious playthings of his brain is in the tune 'Habakkuk' which on close scrutiny, will be seen to be an old French air, which Dr. Hodges adapted to the words, 'Although the vine its fruit deny.' But the Doctor treated this old convivial song with all his contrapuntal skill, preserving its melody, passing it through no less than four distinct modulations, and still without making it difficult to sing.

"The younger organists—those of our day—who know of Dr. Hodges only by hearsay, and think that while he wrote some excellent Church music, he belonged to an antiquated school which had no 'Execution,' know very little about it. Many a young student who scuffles about among the pedals, stumbling around like a blind horse in a grave-yard, should have heard the Doctor's pedal-playing. There was no obscurity about it. Every note was well defined, heel and toe working in good partnership. There was no confusion, no bungling, no uncomfortable correction of false notes. The Doctor, too, was great in musical feats of transposition. He would play a Fugue, the greater Bach in G. minor, or the 'Giant Fugue,' or any others of the old Master, one, two or three tones or semitones higher, and never swerve, or miss a note in manual or pedal.

"But, brought up in the old English school, of which

Arne, Blow, Purcell, Boyce, Walminsley and Gibbons
are exponents, Dr. Hodges did not like Mendelssohn.
The 'Elijah' with its instrumental richness and wonderful dramatic power, did not accord with his musical taste.
He relented somewhat toward the Overture to St. Paul,
because of its dignified treatment of a simple theme, and
fancied the earlier part of the following Fugue ; but had
no sympathy with the rush and orchestral hurry which
bring it to a close.   He would rather play 'We worship
God and God alone' from 'Judas Maccabæus' with its
wonderfully-treated double subjects, than trifle with the
'Lobgesang.'   The Doctor's methods and tastes do not
prevail at present at Trinity, where, while honour is done
to Handel, Mendelssohn and his compeers find happy
representation.

"Inclined to harmony more than melody, his interpretation of the Church Service was admirable.   His pupil,
the late Dr. John Wilcox, used to say, that it was a good
musical education just to hear Dr. Hodges 'give out' a
hymn on the organ; while his accompaniment to the
voice was singularly excellent.   To give an idea of one of
his 'odd ways' of which we have spoken, we may say
that one day, a lady coming out of Church said, 'They
sang that beautiful old tune "Dundee," and the organ
was fine; but I heard all underneath it a sort of small
rolling scale of soft notes, like a gentle sea.   It was away
down under the bass, and seemed like waves breaking
into rock caverns.'   This was one of his peculiar delights.
He had accompanied the voices on the manuals, and,
with the Swell coupled to the Pedals, had produced the
underground murmurs.

"Dr. Hodges had some curious ideas of his own about
the pedals of an organ.

"Nowadays, they are so constructed that unless an
organist is careless there is little need of striking two notes

at once. But the Doctor had the pedals of all organs over which he had control built in the closest possible way, and in addition, had a sort of rail, about the size of a lead pencil, running along the top of each pedal, with a depression in it, so that he could reach over and easily play a Third with the toe. Having charge over all the Trinity Parish organs during his earlier connection with the parish he had them all 'fixed' the same way, which was a very sore discomfiture for the organists of St. Paul's and St. John's, inasmuch as, if they wanted to look at the pedals, they might as well have looked at the rails of a picket fence, they were all apparently alike. He had a peculiar love for Octave Couplers, and for dividing his mixtures into separate ranks, each controlled by its own stop.

"Of Dr. Hodges's compositions it is unnecessary to speak. They are part and parcel of our present sacred musical literature. Himself perfectly acquainted with the structure and capabilities of the organ, an admirable executant, and thoroughly imbued with the true spirit of Church music, he well knew what the organ could do and what it could not do; how far it could be used as an orchestra, and how far it was meant for Church use. Knowing this, and writing in accordance with this knowledge, and with the true Churchman's spirit as well as that of the true Musician, his works are universally recognized as models. Whether in Hymn-tune, Chant or Full Service, they are found everywhere in use, and everywhere standard.

" Dr. Hodges was a musical landmark in his day, the recognized exponent in this city of the highest school of Sacred Music, and an authority among lesser lights.

" His memory is still affectionately cherished by many New Yorkers, and we may only say in concluding this sketch, that doubtless his own words, though jocularly uttered, were true. He was talking with one of his Choristers, just after service, when the latter in parting said : 'Well, good-bye, Doctor, I 'll meet you this afternoon— at any rate in Heaven.'

" 'Very true,' said Dr. Hodges. 'The Psalm says " As well the singers, as the players of Instruments shall be there." '

" G. F. D."

I think G. F. D. must be mistaken about " Habakkuk." Whatever likeness he detects, it is not in the least probable that my Father ever heard the French " Convivial Song."

Also concerning my Father's opinion of Mendelssohn, it is but partially given and probably exaggerated. His words of this, then new, composer, were strictly comparative, not condemnatory. Some years later he enjoyed perusing *Mendelssohn's Letters* immensely, and said to me, " I have a far higher estimation of the man " ; as if he detected in the writer so early taken hence, the refined, thoughtful, and deeply religious musician. I am sure he would have delighted in his Chorales, and in his great dramatic power. Prejudice and narrowness could not exist in my Father's mind, though his convictions were so strong, and his love for the two grand Masters, Handel and Bach, partook of a passionate intensity.

And regarding his pedal playing, my Father would be the last to say he never slipped, but it was such a rare occurrence that it amounted to something very remarkable. In St. John's Chapel his feet could be closely watched as his seat was elevated in the centre of the gallery, and I remember a quaint old Englishman, who officiated as clerk and bass singer, who used to make my Father smile by saying softly, if there was the least indication of a slip, " Aliquando ! " intimating the Latin phrase, " Aliquando bonus dormitat Homerus."

Extract, from an unpublished paper on American church music, during the nineteenth century.

"Some forty years ago, when our church choirs and organists were groping about in musical darkness, and no higher standard of Church Music prevailed than those found in the Tune Books of the day ; when ' Jackson in F ' was supposed to be the *only* setting of the *Te Deum*, as well as the *ne plus ultra* of pure Church Music, and the mere playing it through correctly, a fair test of an organist's skill ; when its use was reserved for the great festivals of the Church, and the expected performance eagerly talked about (weeks in advance) by organists and choirs ; when our prominent musicians were conscious of the debased condition of Church music, yet seemed powerless to make it better ; there arrived in the city of New York, a gentleman bearing a distinguished name,—Edward Hodges, Mus. Doc. of Bristol, England, and holding high rank among the chief musicians of his own country. For a period of more than twenty years, Dr. Hodges not only enjoyed the full confidence and respect of the musical profession, but he also gained many true friends among the clergy and laity of the Church, all of whom appreciated his great talent and high Christian character. During this time, and amid many obstacles, Dr. Hodges worked faithfully and fearlessly, seeking only the improvement and advancement of Church music, and bringing into practice his own sound convictions in regard to the reforms so greatly needed. For over twenty years Dr. Hodges had the direction of the music in Trinity Parish, New York. His first appointment was to St. John's Chapel, in the year 1839, where he remained till the completion of the new Trinity Church in 1846, when he was elected its Organist and Choirmaster. His famous Service (known as 'Hodges in E') was sung for the first time in that Church at the 'Consecration Service,' on 'Ascension Day,' May 21, 1846, and was again performed at the 'Consecration' of Trinity Chapel (the new Chapel of ease to Trinity Church) some eight years later, when Dr. Hodges was appointed Organist and Director of the Choir. England lost what New York gained, in possessing this distinguished musician, and there can be no question that his coming to America was a most fortunate event for our Church Music. He was indeed a Missionary teacher of a purer Musical Gospel than had ever before been preached to our benighted organists and choirs. The good work Dr. Hodges did, more than forty years ago, still lives and bears fruit, as many of his old pupils and disciples can testify ; and the sound musical doctrines which he taught are yet to bloom afresh, when the ignorance and errors that now prevail, shall have passed away. Many will recognize in this sketch an old and valued friend. Others may be told that it refers to the late Edward Hodges, Mus. Doc. of Sydney, Sussex College. Cambridge. He died at Clifton near Bristol, September

1, 1867. 'Blessed are the dead which die in the Lord; even so, saith the Spirit; for they rest from their labours, and their works do follow them.' (Rev. xiv., 13.)

"S. P. T."

The Rev. C. H. Davis, of Littleton Drew, Wilts, writes to the Editor of the *Bristol Mirror*, about 1885 :

" I was interested in your notice of Dr. Hodges, 'A Bristol Worthy.' Some fifty years ago as a boy I was taken to St. James's one Sunday evening, and heard the last Hymn, and I was shown the stately Doctor as he came out, like a D.D. !

" I was told that St. James's Organ was tuned then once a week. The late Canon Havergal used to be Curate at St. James's. In his 'Old Church Psalmody' he gave a C. M. tune adapted by Dr. Hodges from Farrant's Anthem 'Lord for Thy tender mercies' sake,' under the name of 'Farrant,' by Mercer miscalled Gloucester ; and he spoke highly of Dr. Hodges, to whom he was indebted for help in his musical development.

" On the death of Mr. Mutlow in 1832, Dr. Hodges tried for the organist's place in Gloucester Cathedral ; and the late Rev. T. Evans, Master of the College School and Precentor, said that he never heard the accompaniment to the Solos so well done as by Dr. Hodges ; that it was so soft as

scarcely to be heard until the last verse, when
he put on the Swell before the loud Gloria. He
said that the Chapter wished to keep up the *old
connection*, and so elected Mr. Arnott, who had been
Mutlow's pupil.

"Yours truly,

"C. H. D."

A musician, well known in the Church, writes :

"In point of majesty and volume of tone, the
large organ in Trinity Church has no equal in this
country.

"For a period of more than twelve years its
varied powers were developed by the hand of a
Master, and its ample and varied resources not
only displayed (as they have never since been)
but brought under judicious control and management. Indeed your good Father controlled with
a Master's hand every possible effect to be obtained
from Trinity Organ.

"In the days of Old Trinity's musical prosperity
(never to be forgotten) there was a large and efficient choir who sang the grand old Anthems and
Services of Gibbons, Boyce, Purcell, Croft, and
Hodges ; and for the first time in America we
heard the music which has been listened to with
wonder and delight in the daily Cathedral Ser-

vices of the Church of England. But all this has passed away ; and Dr. Hodges has left us to return no more. Yes ; and Trinity Church owed this eminent musician a debt of gratitude for the great and good work he had accomplished in the Parish during the term of his long and faithful service."

CHAPTER XXIII.

THE following interesting extracts are from letters written to me while I was residing in England by my Father's valued and appreciative— and my own much lamented—friend, Dr. S. Parkman Tuckerman.

He lived several years in Switzerland, and loved quaintly to style himself " The Sage of Champéry."

" Vevay, 16 May, 1885.

" Your Father had an awkward and difficult task before him at his trial day at Windsor, and I wonder if you ever thought about it. He came from his CC manual and CCC pedal at St. James's Bristol, to play on an FF manual and pedal, the latter down to FFF. Young Elvey had been brought up on G organs, and of course felt at home with the Chapel organ. However excellent your Father's performances may have been on the trial day, I am sure they would have been still better had the organ been of a compass to which he was accustomed. Dr. Elvey told me years afterwards that he should not dare to play upon a CC manual and pedal at a public perform-ance. There is a class of English musicians who believe that progress means standing still, and holding fast to long-since exploded ideas. Not so your good Father,

who was the first in England to adopt the German organ
compass; and though opposed by the prominent organists (even Samuel Wesley) as well as organ builders, he
won the battle, and lived to see the rapid extinction of
the F and G manuals, and the universal adoption of the
only proper and legitimate compass for the organ. This
was a great triumph for your Father which any musician
might have been proud of."

"*Vevey*, *Jan. 1, 1886.*

"I read the other day an interesting sketch of the life
of Samuel Wesley. He was born in Bristol, as well as
your good Father, though there must have been some
thirty years difference in their ages. As a musician he
was a man of great ability; and no grander piece of pure
Church music was ever written than his 'In Exitu Israel.'
He belongs to the departed great ones; though many at
the present day choose to ignore and forget *him* as well
as others we wot of, who have lived and passed away to a
higher and better life.

"I was much amused at your comparing . . . to a
bare 7th, omitting the 3d and 5th, and you might have
added, without 'preparation' or 'resolution.' Speaking
of 7ths reminds me of an incident that occurred in York
before your Father's decease, and about which I wrote to
him. Dr. Monk saw on my piano a printed copy of
'Hodges in E'; and at my suggestion he took it home to
read at his leisure. A week or so afterward it was returned with a note expressive of pleasure; and he also
said it was the work of a sound Church musician. He
did make exception however, to the consecutive sevenths
which occur at the phrase 'We acknowledge Thee.' I
however took the ground that Dr. Hodges knew what he
was about, and intended to write the passage exactly as
it stands. After this I wrote a little article on the sub-

ject, expressing great admiration for the beautiful effect
produced, notwithstanding that a rule had been set aside
to gain it. It was afterwards printed in one of the London Musical Journals.

" Dr. Stainer some years after, published an Evening
Service with an instance of consecutive sharp sevenths
in the Magnificat ; and the reviewers, one and all, pitched
into him for breaking a recognized musical law. And he
still lives, and the objectional sevenths stand out in his
score as sharply as ever. Sir Walter Scott compared critics
to 'bungling tinkers, who often make more holes than
they mend.' May not this wise saying be aptly applied
to the genus musicâle?"

(There are two examples of consecutive sevenths
in the beautiful Fugue No. 18 of the "48."—F. H.
H.)

I received the following letter from Dr. Parker-
man in answer to one in which I gave my impressions on hearing the "Mass in B minor," by John
Sebastian Bach, at the Royal Albert Hall, London.
I had remarked that at some most impressive and
powerful passages, in the Creed especially, I had
missed the organ pedals ; and my thought reverted
to my Father, whose use of the organ with an orchestra was so remarkably effective.

"In regard to the absence of the pedals 16 and 32 in
certain places in the Mass where the ear not only expected
but yearned for them, the omission of them I think, was
a mere whim of the conductor, and probably Dr. Stainer
had to yield to it. Costa used to do the same thing in a
rough way and would give no reason. In the Chorus

'He sent a thick darkness,' where the pedals are so grandly effective, Costa would say 'I will not allow dat organ to buz so! It is not in de score!' I can readily understand that old memories of your dear Father and his remarkable abilities were suggested by the performance of Bach's great masterpiece. No musician of his day, or even since, had a deeper knowledge or a truer appreciation of the great Cantor than he.

"Bach's 'Forty-eight Preludes and Fugues' (his musical Bible) were his daily study and delight; the well-known volume holding its accustomed place on his grand piano-forte so long as I can remember his study in the house he occupied in Hudson Street.

"That famous book was indeed in my early days a book of mysteries to me and utterly incomprehensible; but to your Father it was his daily musical sustenance; and, coupled with his knowledge of and reverence for Handel, the secret of his great Musicianship.

"The first time I heard, saw, and spoke to Dr. Hodges, was in St. John's Chapel in New York; the year 1840 or 1841. My old teacher Zeuner was with me and we sat in a front pew at the end of the South gallery. After service, Zeuner (who rarely spoke well of any one) said 'Ze Doctare plays finely; we shall go and speak to him'; and we did. How kind and gentle his manner! And how pleased he seemed when I stammered out my thanks, and admiration of his playing, which was a perfect revelation to me and made me cry! Of course my opinion in his eyes could have had but little value, yet it was a sincere appreciation of his talent on my part, so far as I had the musical knowledge to understand him."

"June 27, 1886.

"Many years ago, when in the (to me) sacred precincts of your Father's study in Hudson Street, New York, I asked the good man to tell me why he wrote the first

'Holy' in ' Hodges in C' without a *third*. I cannot re-call his reply at this distant day, yet we both know he did nothing without a reason. My copy of the original score is at home and I cannot refer to it. Can you suggest a reason why Bass and Tenor are thus placed?"

In reply I wrote :

"DEAR DOCTOR :—

"Why 'suggest a reason'?   My Father wrote it. It is bold.   It is very beautiful in its effect ; why say anything further?   The very laws of harmony are sufficient to interpret it.   It was laid hold of by Clarke-Whitfeld in 1825.   He wrote my Father '*I* would not have done it.'   Probably not.   But the young man of twenty-eight whose Doctorate he had done his best to oppose, did it, and saw the force and beauty of it.   It is by such boldness that Musicians teach us.   While some minds are cavil-ling, and others timidly jogging along the beaten track, a musician leaps the barriers.   It seemed most natural for my Father to do it.   To have put the 3d in the second 'Holy' would have made it a common passage at once.   I can never forget the effect produced on my mind by that very passage when I heard my Father render it in Trinity

Church.   There is a silence—and then in the distant, indefinable softness of the organ, the tonic,
fifth and third—the mysterious triad, fall on the
expectant ear.   When the second 'Ter Sanctus'
comes in (*fortissimo*), with full burst, there is a perfect completeness and satisfaction, while the effect
is overpowering.   Only lately I heard Berthold
Tours play it,—and appear to enjoy it,—unques-
tioningly.   In August last I heard the 'Te Deum'
well rendered at Wells Cathedral ; where it is in
constant use and well understood."

My friend continues :

"It seems that I am not the only one who has sought a
reason for the incomplete Triad in your Father's 'Service
in C !'   That *you* have given, is, however, satisfactory, if
it expresses the Composer's views.   At any rate we may
conclude it was done designedly, and for a purpose.
What Dr. Clarke said in reference to it is, and was, of no
consequence.   He wrote heaps of commonplace musical
phrases, both in his Services and Anthems ; the probable
cause of his popularity some sixty years ago.   I remember asking your Father once, why 'Clarke in F' had never
been sung in Trinity Church?   His reply was, 'Look at
the fifth verse' ; where I found the word 'Holy' used
but twice! or else it may have been *four* times; I forget
which.   At any rate *I* corrected the grave error without
tampering with the music, and restored the proper reading."

" Champéry, Valais, July 22, 1886.

"The only information I can give about the Organ in
St. James's Church, Bristol, is from memory.   I saw it

first in 1849, and I remember writing to your Father about its condition about that time. At home I have its full history in type, written I conclude about the time the *new old* Organ was first used, some sixty years ago.

" There was a triple Swell Box, and three sets of thin Venetian Blinds, so called. They were adjusted ingeniously. The first pressure upon the Swell pedal opened the inner blind. The second the middle one, and the third pressure gradually opened the entire Swell. Very grand effects were possible from the Swell manual, if judiciously managed ; and very annoying results followed where a pumping style was adopted. There was a perceptible *hitch* in the Swell pedal as the three sets of blinds were successively opened, and probably this was designed as a guide to the player. The

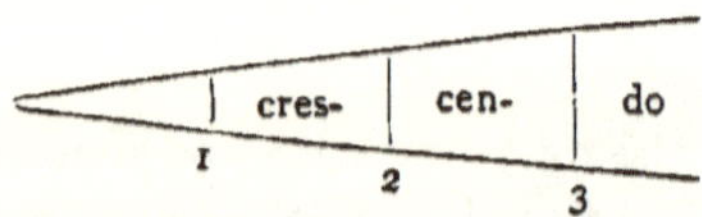

pedal keys were of iron, invented by your Father, and first introduced in this organ. There was a 16 ft. pipe, speaking a 32 ft. tone, but decidedly *fifthy* throughout. The construction was planned and carried out entirely by your Father's direction, and the specification wholly his. It was the first CC Manual and CCC Pedal made in England ; and this ' innovation' (as the fools called it) *originated* with your Father, as far as his own country was concerned.

" The same plans with improvements were adopted in Trinity Church, New York and its Chapel of Ease ; also in St. John's Chapel ; but not in St. Paul's.

" My authority for all I have told you is personal examination of the St. James's organ, and it entirely agrees with the printed account I have at home. Hopkins's History has but a meagre account. The dust and dirt that I accumulated in my two visits to that exalted organ gallery should be sufficient proof that my examination was thorough and my reports correct.

ST. JAMES' CHURCH, BRISTOL.

"I suppose you know that 'Hodges in D' used to be known as the 'New York Service.' And I was told by some one, whom I remember not, that 'Jackson in E flat' being very popular in Trinity Parish, your Father was induced to write a service which should be pleasing and at the same time of a far higher type than Jackson's music, which Jebb calls rowdy and vulgar."

"*Aug. 1st, 1886.*

"Everything and everybody whether musical or otherwise must move in the accustomed grooves or channels in accordance with precedents long established. This you will admit. Therefore can you reasonably expect that the Church Music your good Father left behind him is to come into immediate use, or be received as standard works in the Cathedral and Parish Churches of England? You have done nobly in the good work; and with time and patience your reward is sure to come, though you may not live to see it.

"Could your Father have been persuaded in 1846 to send to England all his Services and Anthems adapted to the English Prayer Book, I believe his music now would be in use, and his name and talents fully recognized and appreciated by the present generation. These appear to be the true reasons why your Father's music is *as yet* coldly received in England, and you must remember that during the last twenty or thirty years, Goss and musicians of his stamp have been pushed aside for younger writers who now possess the popular ear, to the exclusion of the old Cathedral musicians and their successors."

"Your idea of writing your Father's life is a capital one, but I cannot but wonder why you have deferred it so long. You must read my tribute to his memory, for I feel that I knew and appreciated him in the United States better than any one outside his own family.

"When last in Boston, Clarence Dorr, a stock-broker, as well as an enthusiastic lover of Church music met me on State Street, and said to me 'Come into my office, and I will show you something I greatly prize.' He then opened his safe and unlocked a bank trunk, from the bottom of which he brought to light two of your Father's letters dated somewhere in the Forties. I was not asked to read them, but was pleased to find that after so many years had passed, this musical stock-broker continued to cherish his admiration for your Father.

"Dorr used to say we never had but one great organist and thorough Church musician—that was Dr. Hodges."

"*Vevey, Apr. 19, 1886.*

"In reply to your question what were the great leading points in your Father's organ playing, I should answer first, that what he played, how he played and when he played, gave me the impression of a power in reserve, subject to his use when required. He had a clearly de-fined purpose in what he played, and every phrase, chord, or sequence of chords had a meaning. Dr. Hodges's vol-untaries both before and after service might be described as short but complete musical sketches or finished pic-tures, which only a Master's hand and mind could have produced. Yet how few there were amongst the listeners who could appreciate his performance! I remember standing by your Father's side one Sunday morning when he was playing the introductory voluntary. Your brother J. S. B. H. accosted him thus—'Sir, Dr. Berrian seems impatient to begin the service,' and the reply was, 'He must wait until I have finished this phrase.'

"To sum up, Dr. Hodges's organ playing was not only masterly from a musician's standpoint, but it was refined, and in a marked sense that of a Christian gentleman. No one ever heard anything from his hands that could be called common-place or inappropriate for organ use; and when I look back to the New York of forty years ago, Dr. Hodges stood alone, as a bright and shining light amid the musical darkness and ignorance of that period."

Regarding the appointment of organists in cathedrals my friend remarks:

"Fifty years ago (and so it is at the present day) Deans and Chapters required candidates for an organist's position to be *Cathedral-bred.* Their testimonials as to musical ability and good character were (alone) not sufficient. The question was, From which cathedral did you graduate, and, as a chorister, did you serve out your full time? I have not the slightest doubt that your Father would have attained high rank and a cathedral position in England, as he richly deserved, had the days of his boyhood been passed in the choir of Bristol Cathedral.

"Samuel Wesley, with all his remarkable abilities and musical scholarship, was kept out of the cathedrals because not cathedral-bred. Dr. Monk would have been rejected at York for the same reason, had not Sir Frederick Ouseley's great influence and friendship carried him in above all other competitors.

"Why is Sir George McFarren's Church music seldom heard in Cathedral Choirs, or even Parish Churches where good organists and effective choirs exist? Because he received his musical education at the Royal Academy instead of a cathedral, therefore the orthodox character of his music is called in question and for that reason only. One more example and I stop.

"Best told me that years ago he gave up all expectation of obtaining any desirable Church preferment, such as a man of his eminence as an executant and composer entitled him to.　The reason he gave, 'I was not bred in a cathedral; a *sine qua non* for any desirable position.'"

"My correspondence with your good Father taught me how to construct a good letter, which I never learned at school.　His letters upon any and all subjects were perfect models, and ready to put into type the moment they left his pen."

"The gifted Samuel Wesley and his clever and erratic son Sebastian recognized your Father's great abilities; the latter told me as much on my visit to him in Winchester in 1861.　But what can that avail us now?　They have passed within the veil.　There is not one of your Father's contemporaries living but Sir George Elvey, the successful candidate for St. George's Chapel, when your Father was his chief rival at the trial.

"Dr. Hodges was indeed a bright and shining light in his day and generation; a good husband and father, a warm and sincere friend, a learned and accomplished musician, and above all, a devout and sincere Christian, and this is by no means all that might be said of him. Surely, is not the world better for such a life as he lived?

"In giving to the world a Memorial of your dear Father it should be well considered there is danger of overdoing; for a woman's style is always more diffuse than a man's. Forgive me for making these suggestions, and doubt not they come only from the heart, with the desire that your loving task should be successful.

"I am charmed and delighted that our gifted and clever friend, the Rev. J. H. Hopkins has furnished a tribute to your good Father's memory.　Such a testimonial as his pen would furnish would in my eyes be of great value. Dr. Hopkins will remember your Father in the days of his fame and glory; and moreover he was even in those far distant days, musician enough to appreciate your

Father's true missionary work in the Church, and at a period when ' Jackson in F ' and what I might call musical twaddle were generally accepted as true Church music. Plain Song is good in its way; but plain speaking is better when you want to enunciate the truth."

CHAPTER XXIV.

IN reading and copying words written with a deep
love for my Father, by Dr. Tuckerman, I laid
down my pen and fell into a reverie. As I called
up the past and heard again the voices, and even
the foot-falls of so many—so many who were with
me living presences and inspiring minds, as well as
warm personalities, I seemed to lose myself in one
of those surging floods of many memories which at
times sweep over one's soul. Those gone are yet
so near ; their faces seem yet to be only unseen because my eyes are holden. They glide past me and
I realize myself as one standing solitary on an
ocean shore. One by one they have entered the
waiting boat, and pushed away over the chilly waters
in the shimmering gleam towards the distant sunset-
light. " Abii ad plures !" Yes ; the majority are
there ! Of my Father's friends, those who loved
him, some fell in their golden youth, ere the promise
of life was full ; some in manhood ; and some had

reached and gone over the allotted time. All turn
on me a radiant countenance as they pass in memory
before me and seem to say, " But a little while "
(one of the " little whiles of Christ " which I heard
so beautifully brought out by Canon Cross of Chi-
chester) ; " and it is for you to collect the words we
said to you of one who to us was so much, and whose
influence may even now be adding to our happiness in
this, to you at present, unknown life." Who knows ?

I add with pleasure these words, which were written to me on perusal of my manuscript, by a valued
friend, the Rev. J. H. McCracken.

" Snug Harbor, Waterbury, Conn.,
" 20th September, 1894.

" MY DEAR MISS HODGES:

" The last page has been read, not with the care and
time that I should like to have given, but with the sense
of its being a great privilege that I have enjoyed.

" It reminds me of what the present Bishop Nichols, of
California, once said—that he found a good Biography
the most helpful, devotional reading, contrasting it with
other books written to be devotional.

" It is a tonic to come in contact with a strong, buoyant,
devout nature like your Father's ; and his mastery over his
instrument and manly way of acquiring and holding it goes
with one as a beneficent stimulus and guide in one's own life.

" Such, too, may I add, is your own influence, with the
charm added that only personal converse can convey.

" Yours faithfully,

" J. H. McCRACKEN."

And now my book must close, but the subject lies grandly open.

If I were asked where my nearest tie to my Father lies, I should be true in saying, In God's Holy Word, and in the association of it with his own Sacred Music.

Here, he is ever fresh, ever present. It is not that "he *said*" this or that, but "he *is saying it now*."

And is he nearer in this than in the dear remembrance of his face and form? Yes: I think so. It may prove much that was said by our Blessed Lord to His disciples as to His bodily absence, and the power of the Spirit He would send. Of Himself —the earthly part—He had said to one loving soul, "Touch me not." He had gone beyond human love, its imperfections could not reach Him, any more than the clouds which obscure the sun's broad light are near its source.

Thus, the words of Holy Writ, and the parts of our Church Service which my Father chose to weave into the grand harmony of his own spirit, speak with a three-fold power: and bring me nearer to him than any other thought, or scene, or memory, or vision of the night.

Does it seem as if this would be the same with *every* father?

No. I do not think it can be. Music, in the way it occupied his whole mind, was a blending of his intellect, his imagination, his highest powers of thought, with words of Divine Inspiration which have no meaning at all unless they mean *Everything:* everything of real moment which unites the life here with the " Life to come."

And Music, such as he aspired to, such as he imagined, such as he constantly says he desires to join in, is the language of that Life.

> From morning's dawn to setting sun,
> The little span is swiftly run ;
> Its glories, efforts, storms, soon past—
> The evening falls, and Peace at last.

He has passed into the Διατεσσαρον, the realm of perfect accord,

"DEUS NOSTER REFUGIUM,"
being the grand Διαπασον of his life.

From the *Living Church* of March 2, 1895, the editor makes the following extract, as a fitting close to Miss Hodges's devoted filial tribute to her Father.

" No musician of the present time will be more deeply lamented than Miss Faustina Hasse Hodges, who departed this life in the city of Philadelphia, on Feb. 4th. Up to the very eve of her illness, she had devoted her life to the study and practice of her musical art with unabated vigor and enthusiasm. She composed freely and with a grace of feeling which none who ever heard her compositions could forget. Who ever heard her beautiful ' Rose Bush,' or ' Dreams,' or her 'Suffer little children, each one so full of sentiment and feeling, without the thought that its author was wellnigh inspired? Her interpretations of Bach's Fugues and other recondite forms of classic art, were a daily delight to her choice circle of friends and musical admirers. The past few years of her life had been largely devoted in preparing for publication a volume of memorial studies from the life of her distinguished father, Dr. Edward Hodges, the founder and illustrious representative of the Anglican cathedral school of music in the American Church. The memory of his twenty-five years' faithful service in Trinity parish, New York, survives in vivid remembrance as the earliest and, as yet, most splendid period in the annals of our musical liturgies. No greater example of true and faithful filial devotion ever lived than this daughter. She has gone to her rest."

THE END.